An introduction to

HANG GLIDING

by Bob Mackay

Published by
Thornhill Press
24 Moorend Road
Cheltenham
Glos.

ISBN 0 904110 92 3

Printed by
R. J. Washington
Southwood Lane
Cheltenham

CONTENTS

The Author wishes to acknowledge the help given by Pat King Chairman of the B.H.G.A. 1977/78 and Tony Fuell from the Editorial Board of WINGS! in shaping the text; John Ievers Managing Director of Hiway Hang Gliders Ltd, and Len Gabriels Managing Director of Skyhook Sailwings Ltd for their historical records and advice on Powered Hang Gliders; Mark Junak who took almost all the photographs and Tony Tate who did the illustrations.

Front cover: Mick Maher flying the Southdown Sailwings' 'LIGHTNING' in the 1981 Manufacturers Competition at Hay Bluff, Powys, Wales.   (Photo by Mark Junak)

INTRODUCTION

Although this book is primarily intended for those who want to learn to fly, it is also written to be understood by the interested onlooker. If you enjoy watching Hang Gliding it will add a great deal to your pleasure. There *are* technical passages essential to the prospective pilot, but you need not dwell on them to understand the general description. Hang Gliding suffered from cheap sensational treatment by the media in its early days. Most of the general public have a totally false idea of what it's all about. In the same way, early attempts at aviation are often depicted by speeded up comic clips of film showing exploding rockets and flapping monstrosities shaking themselves to pieces. These were the ill-conceived attempts of fools and an insult to the years of patient work by people like Lilienthal, who built and flew the first Hang Gliders in the 1890's and the Wright brothers from 1900 to 1910 developing powered aircraft. Learning to fly has always required a great deal of dogged, patient, careful determination and this is far more characteristic of Hang Gliding than of any other form of flying.

So often one hears people say . . . "It's far too dangerous for *me*.", when the truth is quite the reverse . . . it is *they* who are far too dangerous for *it*. The idea that some things are dangerous and others safe is a fallacy. Danger is a product of human carelessness, inexperience and ineptitude. If statistics are anything to go by we make most of it on our roads and in our kitchens. Some people are more accident prone than others no matter what they are doing. You will bring your own danger into the sport and if you can't accept that, don't take up Hang Gliding.

CAN ANYBODY DO IT? Almost . . . it does not take more than a few hours to learn the basics of controlling a Hang Glider. It's no more difficult than learning to ride a bicycle. Any fool can fly one . . . but not for very long! When you take off in a Hang Glider you are completely on your own. Only your skill is looking after you . . . nothing else.

You have to come to terms with fear. Suddenly faced with the unexpected all pilots experience fear but they are not 'gripped' by it so they cease to function. Rather the opposite, their concentration is sharpened, awareness heightened and reactions quickened. You are a long way towards not being inhibited by fear if you will just recognise it for what it is ... part of a natural body reaction 'keying you up' for an exceptional effort. There is no reason to be ashamed of it, don't let it put you off, don't suppress it ... use it.

You must also acquire a thorough understanding of how air behaves as it moves over hill and plain. We can't see it but we can feel it, measure its changes and observe its effects. Smoke, trees, water, crops, birds and the sound of the wind around familiar objects, are all indicators. We study the weather and watch the clouds (endlessly). We know their different shapes and what makes them so . . . You have to learn how to read the sky.

WHAT'S IT LIKE? The book tells you all about the agonising frustrations and fierce joys of learning but it can only give you an inkling of what it feels like to float high over hill and plain. Listening to your favourite music can come somewhere near it, but it lacks the intensity, the reality, the transcending of normal human experience that comes from seizing the gift of wings and flying. Hang Gliding is its purest form . . . there is no cockpit, no engine, no controls; the glider becomes part of you and you soar like an eagle (a rather busy, slightly less than supremely confident, occasionally very anxious eagle, but none the less like an eagle for all that). I have piloted a fair number of aircraft, some like the Spitfire and the Tiger Moth the finest of their type, but for real flying . . . give me a Hang Glider every time.

CHAPTER 1
THE HANG GLIDER

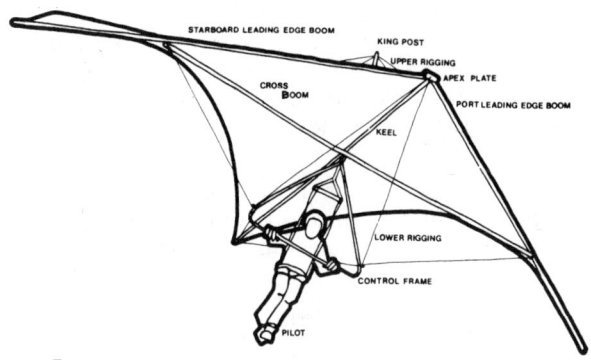

Figure 1. The Rogallo Sailwing

This is the design developed from Dr. Francis Rogallo's original concept in the U.S.A. during the 60's, hence the caption the Rogallo Sailwing or more affectionately a 'Bog Standard Rog' which we all flew until about 1975. The two leading edge spars were set at an angle of 80 degrees bisected by the keel. These supported a simple kite-like sail arched in the form of twin cones. In the air, it was so inherently stable that it took a major effort to make it change attitude and turn. On the ground, it was difficult to keep the nose at just the right angle so that taking off was always a critical manoeuvre.

It didn't need a professor in aerodynamics to point the way development had to go . . . just take a look at any soaring bird. Long narrow wings are far more efficient for gliding. The Albatross can remain airborne for days on no more than the lift from wind over wave. Its wing has a span of nearly12ft and a chord (front edge to back edge) of about 1ft. We divide one by the other to produce a figure we call the Aspect Ratio, in this case 12. The A/R of the old 'Bog Rog' was less than 4 and a really steep slope was needed to get it off the ground.

We have come a long way since then, through five so called 'generations' of development. The classifications are a little artificial since advances by one manufacturer have overlapped another and different avenues have been explored. We can best follow the 'mainstream' by looking at the successive models of one major British manufacturer, Hiway Hang Gliders Ltd., of Tredegar.

The photographs show how design has developed but what has this given us in terms of performance? Here are a selection of milestones in achievement.

Date	Pilot	Glider	Flight
Nov 1972	Nick Regan	Home built Rogallo	First Hang Glider flight in the U.K.
July 1976	Bob Calvert	Hiway Cloudbase	7 miles. First cross country flight recorded.
Aug 1976	Kevin Jordan	Hiway Cloudbase	Remained airborne for 12hrs 15 mins in ridge lift.
May 1977	Nigel Milnes	Phoenix 6 B	22 miles cross country
Oct 1978	Geoff Snape	Flexiform Vector	27 miles cross country
	Bob Calvert	Hiway Superscorpion	30 miles cross country
	Bob Bailey	La Mouette Atlas	30 miles cross country
May 1979	Bob Bailey	Birdman Cherokee	50 miles cross country
May 1980	Peter Hargreaves	"	69 miles cross country
Aug 1980	Bob Calvert	La Mouette Atlas	79 miles cross country
April 1981	John Stirk	Solar Wings Typhoon	83 miles cross country

The CLOUDBASE (1976). Nose angle increased to 90 degrees. Sail battens near the wing tips to improve aerodynamic efficiency. Deflexor struts and wires to prevent the longer and more heavily stressed leading edges from bending (second generation).

The SCORPION (1977). Nose angle increased to 112½ degrees. Embryonic keel-fin made necessary for directional stability by the wider nose angle. Sail fully battened (embryonic third generation).

The SUPERSCORPION (1978). Nose angle 120 degrees. Fully developed keel-fin configuration giving 'flexwing' control (see Chap. 6). The deflexors are gone, the leading edges are more strongly built and designed to bend slightly. The sails are specially cut to work with them and are fully battened (third generation proper).

The VULCAN (1980). Nose angle 128 degrees. Leading edge pocket increased producing the beginnings of a double surfaced aerofoil (fourth generation).

*The DEMON (1981). Nose angle 125 degrees (slightly reduced
from the previous model). Leading edge pocket extended
back to produce a 60% double surface wing. Plastic foam
and pre-formed battens are used to produce a much more
sophisticated aerofoil section. The crosstube is no longer
rigidly fixed to the keel but 'floats' inside the double surface
(fifth generation).*

The SIGMA (1980), a no-crossboom design by Southdown Sailwings of Hove.

Parallel development has taken place in gliders with no crosstube, the keel being extended forward to support the leading edges with wires.

The Hang Glider of today has become a cleverly designed yet relatively simple aircraft that can be transported on the roof of a car, carried to the take-off point by one person, rigged and foot launched to fly over 100 miles. (The world record now, 1981, is approaching 200 miles). Flights that were considered exceptional in 1978 are now commonplace and are the normal expectation of the average pilot. Unlike the high performance sailplane, a Hang Glider can be safely landed in a field not much larger than a football pitch. This means that there is far more scope for the pilot to venture wide and high when conditions are suitable.

The SEALANDER (1981), an innovative design by Flexiform Skysails of Manchester . . . just maybe the birds have got it right after all.

CHAPTER 2
HOW DOES IT FLY

If you move a curved surface (aerofoil) through still air angled slightly to your direction of travel the

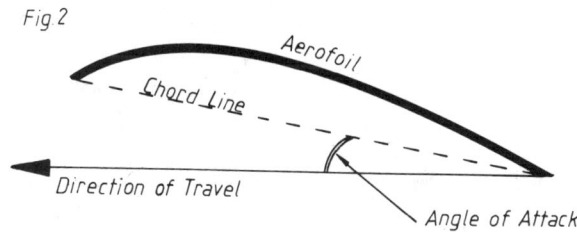

Fig. 2

Aerofoil

Chord Line

Direction of Travel

Angle of Attack

underside will push air downwards causing an increase in pressure underneath. The upper surface will pull air downwards causing a reduction in pressure above. The faster you go the greater the difference producing a greater upward force we call LIFT. The build-up of pressure below the wing forces some air to accelerate around the leading edge. This produces a reduction in pressure there as well as above, so that the overall lift force acts slightly forward rather than straight up.

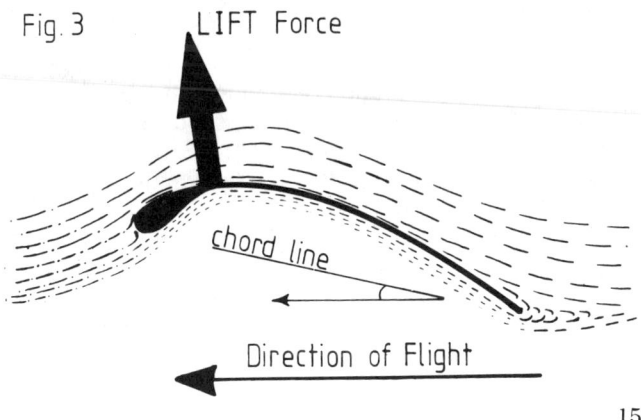

Fig. 3

LIFT Force

chord line

Direction of Flight

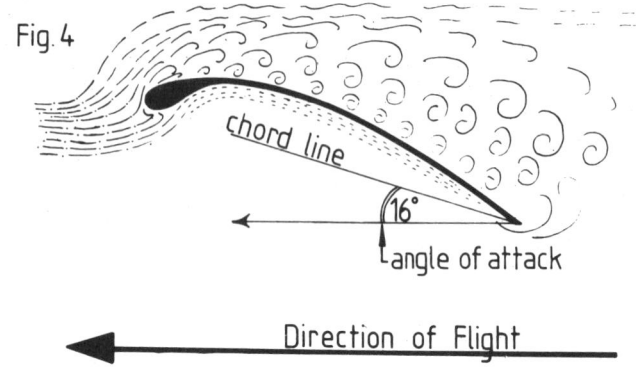

Fig. 4

chord line

16°

angle of attack

Direction of Flight

We can also increase lift by increasing our angle of attack. This can be achieved smoothly up to approx. 16 degrees. Above this angle, air can no longer be induced to flow smoothly and becomes turbulent. The pressure reduction above the wing is lost and with it more than half our lift. We describe this transition as STALLING.

The other aerodynamic force acting on the wing is DRAG. It occurs in two ways:-

1) From the resistance of the air to anything passing through it, a fact readily appreciated by anyone riding a bicycle in a strong headwind. It is the product of frontal area, shape and surface texture, hence the cyclist bends low to reduce frontal area and wishes he had a streamlined smooth shape. The resistance increases with speed and is called FORM DRAG.

2) The second is more easily understood by illustration.

The slower we fly (increasing the angle of attack), (Fig. 5), the more developed the vortices become, creating more resistance. This we term INDUCED DRAG.

The relationship for a typical training glider is shown in Fig. 6 (The figures approximate to those for a heavy pilot in full flying kit, 190lbs, flying seated and a glider weight of 50lbs.

Fig.5 <u>Continuous</u> lines show airflow **over** the wing induced inwards by reduced pressure.

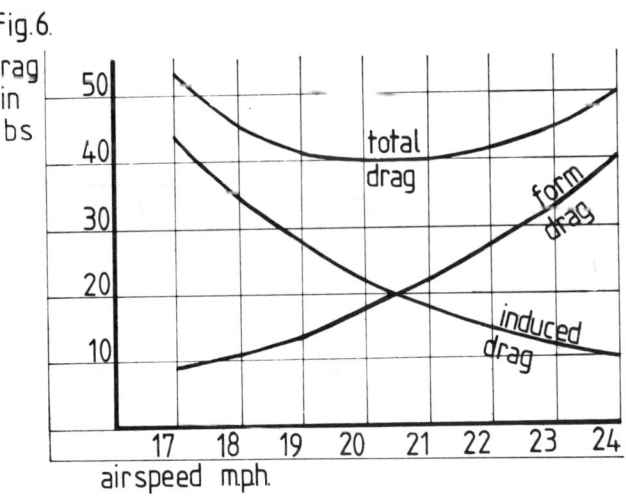

Dotted lines show airflow **under** the wing deflected outwards by increased pressure.

The conjunction of angled flows produces vortices along the trailing edge, with the tip ones largest.

Total drag is lowest at an airspeed between 20 and 21 mph. We will come back to this and its significance in overall performance in Chapter 8.

Fig.6.

drag in lbs

total drag

form drag

induced drag

airspeed m.p.h.

CONTROLLING THE HANG GLIDER

To fly through the air we must use the lift force generated by the wing to do a lot more than just keep us up. It also has to overcome drag *and* take us in the direction we want to go. Level flight relative to the ground is achieved when the air is flowing up the hill at the same speed and angle as the glider is flying down through it. Imagine you are walking *down* an escalator that is going *up* and you will get the idea. The pilot is attached to the control frame by his harness straps which are vertical and he is holding the control bar comfortably in front of him in the 'Piano player' position. The lift pulling upward and forward, coupled with his weight pulling downward, acts like a tensioned bowstring producing a forward force overcoming drag.

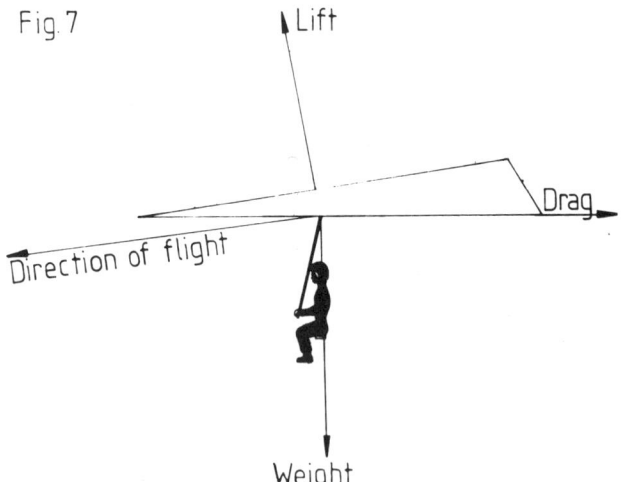

Fig. 7 — Lift, Drag, Direction of flight, Weight

If the pilot pulls on the control bar, he shifts his weight forward relative to the glider. This upsets the balance and the nose drops. The wing is now inclined so that the lift is pulling more forward, the angle of attack is reduced and the glider's speed through the air increases. If the pilot pushes his weight backwards the opposite effect is achieved—the nose goes up, the angle of attack is increased and the glider's speed through the air decreases. Alteration to the position of the nose, up and down, are termed PITCHING movements. You will notice that we have not said that the glider ascends or descends. This is deliberate since whether or not you go up or down, relative to the ground, depends on the speed of the wind and the steepness of the slope over which you are flying. It is these factors in relation to your airspeed that determine whether you ascend or descend. Imagine yourself on that upgoing escalator again. If you walk down slowly enough you will actually be going up.

A well trimmed glider will assume its normal flying attitude, adopting its designed angle of attack, when no pressure is applied to the control bar. It follows therefore that you keep pulling your weight forward to sustain increased airspeed and keep pushing it back to sustain reduced airspeed. Obviously you can overdo either and eventually fly into the ground or stall. The movements are small, only a matter of inches, and the pressures are moderate.

TURNING, We have to incline or BANK the wing so

Fig 8a. Initiating the turn:

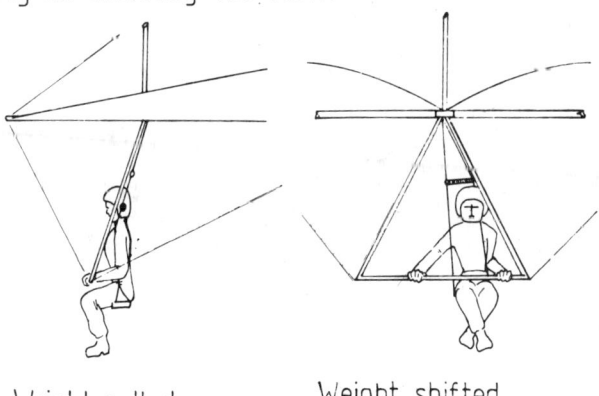

Weight pulled forwards.

Weight shifted sideways.

that the lift force is pulling in the direction we wish to turn (as well as upwards and forwards). We are requiring the wing to do more work i.e. produce more lift so we must increase speed. To simply increase the angle of attack would be to approach the STALL, dangerously reducing our safety margin. We always increase speed i.e. reduce the angle of attack going into a turn. There is also the added bonus that speed makes the glider more responsive to control movements. Speed is safety!

The pilot first pulls his weight forward and then moves himself sideways (Fig. 8a). This produces an increase in speed and causes the wing to drop on the side to which the weight has been shifted. The glider now starts to BANK; as the lift starts pulling in the direction he wishes to go the glider starts to turn. If the pilot kept his weight forward and off centre he would continue to increase speed and angle of bank and the turn would steepen into a spiral dive. Once into the turn, centrifugal force tends to return the pilot to the central position, weight is then shifted to maintain a constant angle of bank and airspeed.

Fig. 8b. Maintaining the turn.

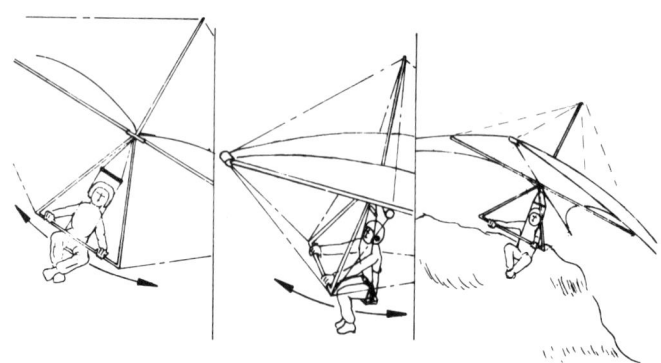

Weight shifting to maintain a constant angle of bank and airspeed.

To come out of the turn, speed is again increased and then weight shifted to bring the wings level. Once this has been achieved speed can be reduced until the control bar is at the normal flying speed position. Alterations banking the wing we term ROLLING movements. We will be looking at turns in more detail in later chapters.

PILOT HARNESSES. Until 1980 the majority of schools used the seated harness (illustrated in Figs. 8a and b) for teaching beginners. There is now, however, a growing tendency to use a prone harness adjusted to a head up legs down position (referred to as 'budgie') for first 'hops'.

'Budgie' on a VORTEX 120, manufactured by The Chargus Gliding Co. Ltd. of Buckingham.

Note how the trailing edges of the wing twist upwards towards the wingtips. Glider;—An ATLAS by Mouette of France. Pilot:- Bob Bailey.

In this attitude the absolute beginner is less likely to allow the bar position to get too far forward and inadvertently stall. It also prevents another common fault seated pupils have, of swinging their legs forward as they round out from the descent i.e. 'flare' to touch down. This shifts weight forward reducing the effectiveness of the flare and results in the pupil 'ploughing' to a standstill on his backside.

'Budgie' has some snags, the pupil needs to transfer his hands in flight from the control bar to the uprights to achieve a full flare. If he doesn't and lands a little fast or awkwardly, he tends to pitch forward; hence the wheels fitted to the control bar.

There is some restriction in lateral movement so that a return to the seated position is desirable when you start doing prolonged descents and practising turns. Later, as you approach the soaring stage you may wish to use a progressively adjusted prone harness to avoid the traumatic experience of converting from seated to fully prone as described in Chapter 8.

Whichever method you choose it will not alter the **basic techniques** of flying as outlined in later chapters.

STABILITY. The ability of the glider to fly itself with no control inputs by the pilot.

PITCH STABILITY. The 'twist' in each wing (see photograph) reduces the angle of attack towards the tips. This is called 'washout'. A slight reflex is also introduced at the trailing edge of the wing near the centre. These areas are well back and in line with the direction of flight (at zero angle of attack). They work like the feathers on a dart (or arrow) damping any tendency for the nose to pitch up and down.

ROLL STABILITY. The pilot accounts for some 4/5ths of the total weight and in his low-slung position exercises a pendulum effect whenever he 'locks' his position to the control bar.

Each wing can be angled to the horizontal termed 'dihedral'. The righting action results from the differences in angle of attack created when the banked glider starts to slip sideways.

Fig. 9. Roll. stability.

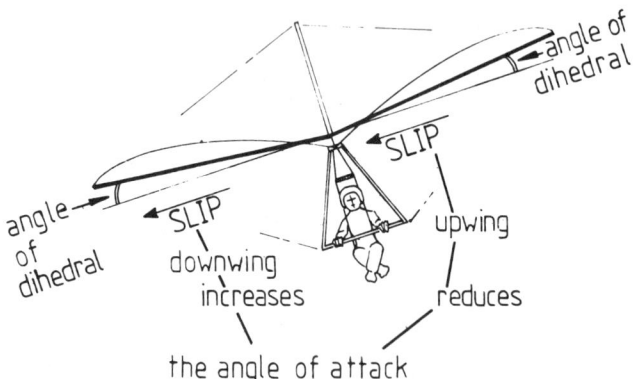

These methods are used to damp and correct any tendency the glider has to roll.

YAW OR DIRECTIONAL STABILITY. Any movement of the nose to one side or other of the line of flight when the glider is flying wings level we term yaw. It is restrained by the swept back wing configuration. A yaw moves one wingtip outwards and the other inwards. Total drag is offset and this *coupled with the 'weathercock' action of the keel pocket (or fin)* tends to pull the nose back in line damping the tendency to yaw (Fig. 10).

The designer tries to give us just enough stability in PITCH, ROLL and YAW so that in good conditions we can relax and let the glider fly itself. However, in difficult conditions or crowded airspace, too much built in stability makes for hard and tiring work. Some earlier high performance gliders were notoriously 'heavy' in roll, others were far too 'light' in pitch. One

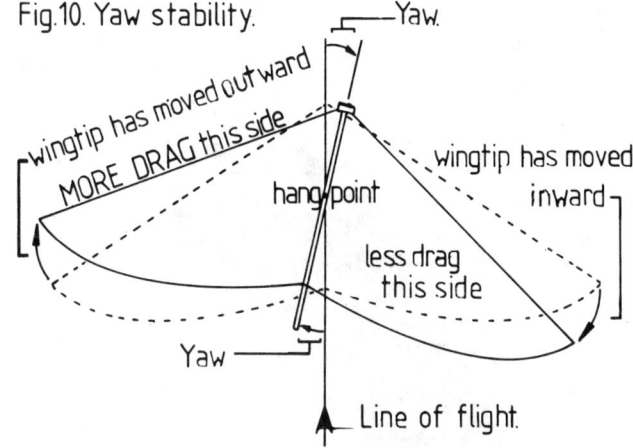

Fig.10. Yaw stability.

or two 'sweet' handling gliders only achieved it at the expense of glide angle performance. As the art of designing has progressed ingenuity has taken place of compromise so that we are now getting some 'sweet' handling high performance gliders.

So far we have considered only stability in flight. No less important is the ease of handling on the ground and during take off.

TAKE OFF STABILITY. Standard Rogallos present the beginner with considerable difficulty in holding the correct attitude (angle of attack) during the take of run. With the development of pre-formed sail battens, built in trailing edge reflex and 'stiffer' sails this problem has virtually disappeared. You will notice in the majority of take off situation photographs, that the glider is obviously holding the correct attitude on its own, the pilot is only applying a *forward* pressure through the uprights of the control frame. If you are about to learn on a glider which has this characteristic you will be able to modify your take off method accordingly.

GROUND HANDLING STABILITY. The more flexible or 'floppy' the wing the more difficult it will be to control it during ground handling. Some of the earlier keel pocketed wings with flexible battens were real 'pigs' to manoeuvre on your own. You had to have a wing man on one side at least. Again, the more modern 'stiffer' sails ground handle more easily.

The SABRE (1981), a fifth generation high performance glider produced by Skyhook Sailwings of Oldham. Pilot: Jim Brown.

CHAPTER 3
AIR MOVEMENT and SITE ANALYSIS

Your early flying will always be close to the ground (below 600ft) in air that is being forced to rise over a hill or ridge. It is therefore essential to have a thorough understanding of how various features affect the flow of air over them. No two sites are alike and none absolutely perfect . . . gulleys, spurs and upwind terrain all cause different problems as the wind speed and direction changes from hour to hour. The basic principles are described in this chapter and then amplified through the book but you never stop learning. No matter how experienced a pilot becomes you will always see him seek advice from local flyers before flying a strange site for the first time.

If you watch the clouds rising from a cooling tower or smoke from a large fire you will begin to get some idea of how air behaves. Once moving it seldom flows smoothly, being easily disturbed by ground features and changes in temperature. Swirls, billows and waves develop readily and persist far longer than you would expect.

These effects are less pronounced on coastal sites. The sea maintains an even temperature and is free from obstructions so that a reasonably stable air mass flowing off it onto a coastal ridge produces very smooth flying conditions i.e. no TURBULENCE.

Let's take ourselves to two types of coastal soaring sites on a good day, wind blowing 'straight on' (at right angles to the ridge or cliff) at 16mph. If we lie down on the face of the ridge amid grass and gorse we shall feel very little wind at all. If we sit up we feel a gentle breeze on our face. When we stand up we begin to feel something of the real wind but we should have to climb a pole to a height of 50—100ft directly above where we are standing in order to experience its full effect.

This increase in wind speed with distance away from the ground we term WIND GRADIENT.

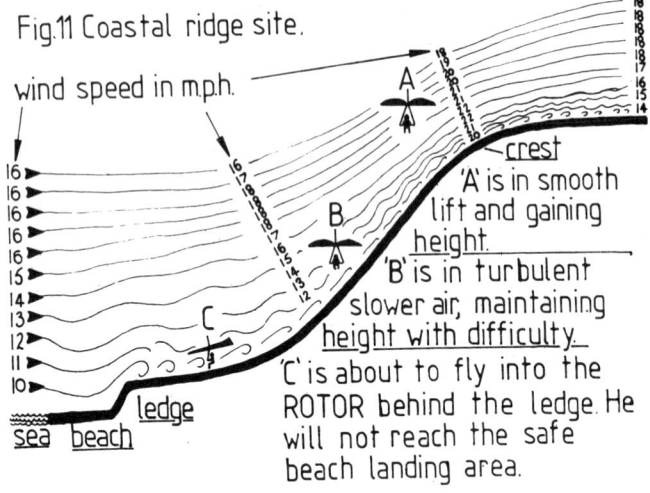

Fig.11 Coastal ridge site.

wind speed in m.p.h.

'A' is in smooth lift and gaining height.

'B' is in turbulent slower air, maintaining height with difficulty.

'C' is about to fly into the ROTOR behind the ledge. He will not reach the safe beach landing area.

POINTS TO NOTE
1. How the airstream is accelerated in passing over the crest. Do not confuse this with wind gradient.
2. How the wind gradient is 'compressed' at the crest reaching 20 mph only 8—10ft above the ground.
3. How turbulence is developing behind the crest as the air leaves the 'smoothing' effect of the accelerated zone and begins to slow down.
4. How the airstream is reversed behind the sharp edge of the lower ledge. This we term ROTOR EFFECT. It is the pitfall for more injuries than almost any other single feature of air movement.

It is fairly easy for you to examine ROTOR EFFECT for yourself. Simply stand a little way back from the crest of any ridge on a windy day and you will find spots where you can hardly feel any wind at all. If the crest is a sharp edge, you may find places where the wind is blowing in the opposite direction. The effect is even more marked at the top of cliffs. Only experienced pilots should attempt cliff soaring.

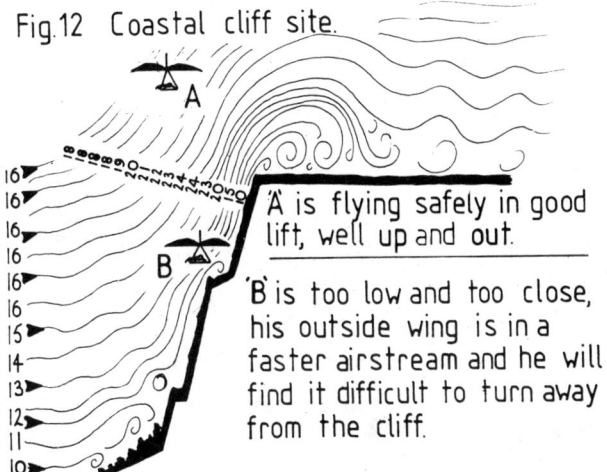

Fig.12 Coastal cliff site.

'A' is flying safely in good lift, well up and out.

'B' is too low and too close, his outside wing is in a faster airstream and he will find it difficult to turn away from the cliff.

POINTS TO NOTE
1. How the flow is slightly more accelerated in front of the top.
2. How the wind gradient alters rapidly.
3. There is a 'dead' zone at the foot of the cliff where the air movement is completely unpredictable. Landing on a narrow beach at the foot of a cliff when the wind is straight on is asking for trouble.
4. How the rotor effect is more severe.

INLAND the same air mass will be travelling slower and will have developed some turbulence. (Fig. 13).

Again we illustrate air movement 'frozen' at a moment in time. The turbulence within the general air mass is not strong, only about 2—3mph in the direction of the arrows. The whole mass however is moving across the landscape at 14mph. Over the crest of the ridge it is to some extent 'smoothed' and accelerated to 16mph. The effect of the turbulence will be gusts up to 19mph and lulls down to 13mph. A glider flying in these conditions would not be slammed about like a power boat in a rough sea. Air is much less dense.

Fig.13
Inland turbulence.

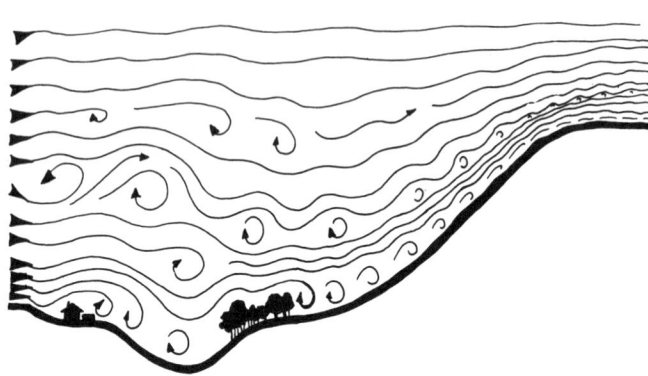

Watching the flying, we would see pilots making small corrective movements to maximise the 'ups' and minimise the 'downs'. 'Ups' you ride as long as you can, gaining as much height as possible—'downs' you get out of—fast! The conditions are well within the limits of our control capability and would be described as reasonably good but a bit 'bumpy'.

POINTS TO NOTE

1. Buildings, hollows or woods create marked leeward rotor effects. Keep well away.

2. The air above and downwind is also affected for a considerable distance. Keep plenty of extra speed on when flying in turbulence close to the ground.

3. Flying well out from the ridge you would find 'lift' or 'sink' between 150—250ft per min for short periods. In the 'smoothing' effect of the ridge it will be less dramatic.

4. We have omitted thermal activity which is covered in Chapter 9.

Whilst our illustration may appear slightly exaggerated to make its points, it would certainly be accurate if the general air mass were moving at 20—22mph (26—28 on the crest). Wave and rotary turbulence within it could be 4—6mph in any direction, more if the site were affected by some particularly nasty upwind feature. Lulls down to 20 mph and gusts up to 34 mph would be felt on the crest. These are conditions for experienced pilots only. They are still within our control capability but a thorough knowledge of the site and a complete familiarity with the glider is needed to handle them. For the less experienced a good rule is: don't fly when the variations in windspeed are more than 5 mph each way.

Visible evidence of how turbulence behaves over the face of the ridge can readily be observed in the patterns of gusts spilling onto sheltered water or travelling across standing crops. They can strike and fan out or roll along like waves momentarily reversing or accentuating the wind gradient (See Chapter 8.) There are a reasonable number of inland sites with few if any 'nasty' features which on good days can be no more demanding than coastal sites. Start, by flying good sites on good days. As your skill develops you will be able to cope with more difficult sites in more varied conditions.

CHAPTER 4
FIRST STEPS

It has been, and to some extent still is, a popular misconception that this is a sport for the rugged individualist—the lone spirit, free as a bird . . . This is a myth! As in any other sport where the consequences of a mistake can be serious—(Sub-Aqua, Mountaineering and Pot holing)—learning is a very exacting discipline. It is not something to be attempted on you own. Contrary to another popular misconception, the first requirement of a pilot is *not* superb reactions, split second timing, fearless courage etc., etc.,—IT IS DISCRETION.

Send a large stamped addressed envelope together

with a cheque or P.O. for 30 pence (1981) to the British Hang Gliding Association, 167a Cheddon Road, Taunton, Somerset to obtain their latest information pack. (Outline of the sport, lists of schools and clubs, list of books and a copy of the monthly journal Wings!). Contact your nearest club and arrange to spend a few days on the hills with them. Don't expect to be greeted with open arms—'many are called but few are chosen'. Chat up any club official, preferably the club Coach or Instructor if they have one. No matter what you see others do, never address yourself to a pilot who is rigging or preparing to take off. Pick one who has just landed and is obviously free to talk to you. Show you are genuinely interested and keen to learn to fly and you will invariably get a friendly response. Help carry a glider or two and you will be enthusiastically adopted. Information is hard to come by. It takes time. Don't make-up your mind too quickly, you may have chosen a good day (or a bad one).

If you are (still) determined to learn to fly then the best way is to go to a good school. The advantages are:-

1. They can operate over a wider range of conditions (using tethered methods and experienced supervision) than you would be able to cope with doing it any other way.
2. You don't have to buy a glider and if you bend theirs it doesn't cost you any more.
3. If you find, (and 95% do), that it is not quite what you expected—well at least you can say that you have actually flown a hang glider (and survived) and you didn't waste a lot of money buying one.

Make sure the school is B.H.G.A. registered. The association has set standards and has a full time Training Officer who inspects and monitors registered schools. Any not maintaining the required standards are promptly de-registered. A sure guarantee of registration is that the school is able to issue Pilot One certificates to student pilots reaching the standards laid down in the B.H.G.A. Pilot Rating scheme. If it can't it isn't a registered school!

There are a wide variety of schools from the large with several instructors and alternative facilities if the weather is unsuitable, to small 'two-man operations' who limit their number of students. Schools can vary with changes of staff. You need to choose carefully. try to visit them before you 'sign on' and see how they operate. If you want to progress beyond 'ground hops' you must be prepared to attend for at least two or three weekends. Conditions may be unfavourable and flying may not always be possible. It can be expensive, so read the small print about refunds.

There *are* Non-Registered Schools, mostly small single handed operators taking one or two pupils only at a time. If the operator is not a B.H.G.A. Qualified Instructor my advice to you is *have nothing to do with him*. Rare exceptions have taught people successfully one at a time, being very selective of conditions and fairly thorough, but you have to make your own assessment of them which you are not qualified to do. They could easily be 'ripping you off' and risking your neck at the same time. There's no guarantee.

Alternatively, you can join a club which has a B.H.G.A. qualified instructor. Much will depend on how far you have to travel to sites in their control and the number learning. You will have to buy a training glider if the club has not got one (few have). However, if you do, you will get a fair amount of individual attention and if your progress is slow it will not cost you any more. We have 6 or 7 members in our local club who started this way and are now fairly expert pilots. About 6-8 months from start to regular soaring is average. It all depends on access to good sites and weather conditions.

Although the outlay on a second hand glider may be £250—£300 and membership of the club and B.H.G.A. £20—£30, there are advantages.
1. You can proceed at your own pace.
2. You will experience club life, learning a lot both on and off the hill. You will also be receiving the

Association's monthly journal Wings!

3. If you do change your mind you can always sell the glider and may be less out of pocket than going several times to a school.

Two things you must have . . . a car and a telephone. You have to be 'in' on the morning liaison about conditions and which site to go to. You also have to be able to get there and wait for conditions to become suitable for your limited experience. This may not occur until late in the day. Sharing vehicles, depending on others, leads to bad decisions, bent gliders and broken bones.

Jenny Ganderton, winner of the Women's Competition, April 1981. Her glider is a TYPHOON (fifth generation design) from Solar Wings of Marlborough, the same type as that used to establish a new British record of 83 miles (see Chap. 1).

However if you are female and something less than an Amazon you will need help. Even the smallest glider is going to weigh over 35lbs and has to be carried up the hill several times. You would not be considering taking up the sport if you didn't think that you can do anything a man can do (and a few things he can't). Great, . . . but don't let your determination to prove it cloud your discretion. You do have physical limitations which mean that you will need more time to accomplish each step and it may take as much as a year for you to become a soaring pilot. I hope you do.

CHAPTER 5

BUYING A HANG GLIDER

Add the weight of the glider to your own weight in full kit. This figure in lbs equals the largest wing area in square feet that you should attempt to fly. i.e. your WING LOADING should not be less than one lb per sq. ft. (5Kg per sq. metre). Being over-weight is no great disadvantage when you have experience to compensate for it. One or two of us are flying with wing loadings up to 1.4 lbs per sq. ft. but for learning 1.1 to 1.2 lbs. sq. ft. is ideal. New gliders are all sold with recommended pilot weights quoted for each model.

Forget about 'generations' in the advancing design of gliders. Whenever you take up the sport there will be three distinct stages in learning, roughly corresponding to the B.H.G.A. Pilot Rating Scheme:-
Student to Pilot One . . . . Training Glider.
Pilot One to Pilot Two . . . . Intermediate Glider.
Pilot Two to Pilot Three . . . . Advanced Glider.

Why shouldn't I buy an Intermediate glider to start? (Oh, I can see we are going to have trouble with you all through the book) . . . Because . . . when you are learning, you either put too little or too much into your control movements. You need more stability and 'forgiveness' built into the glider. What you don't need is performance which can suddenly put you 50ft above where you expected to be, needing a steep 'S' turn (which you don't know how to do) to get into the landing area. Or . . . having made a good straight descent (a little too fast), you find the glider showing no inclination to slow down and lose height as you overshoot the landing area . . . think about it!

The Manufacturer and your club will advise you and it will do no harm to find out what type of glider the local schools are using. There are several manufacturers who produce 'Trainers' and there are independant stockists who sell several types and will advise you. All advertise in Wings! There is also a **British Hang Glider Manufacturers** Federation (B.H.G.M.F.) who have closely co-operated with the B.H.G.A. to produce an Airworthiness Scheme. From 1981 most gliders will be sold with a Certificate of Conformity for their type, one of which will have been put through the Airworthiness Tests. This, apart from being re-assuring, also enhances the resale value.

Secondhand gliders abound.! You do not know enough to buy one on your own. Take an experienced pilot or better still, your Club Safety Officer with you when you go to buy. Having bought it, get it checked over by the Safety Officer or the original manufacturer, particularly if it is an 'old standard'.

Don't think you cannot progress to soaring on your Trainer. Soaring is far more a matter of good conditions on good sites than actual glider performance. In 1974 one hour flights were commonplace on old 'Bog Rogs' with glide angles of one in five. Today's Trainers have better performances than that.

Every brand new glider has an information booklet which contains notes on rigging. Find a sheltered spot, well away from the flying, and practise rigging, de-rigging and packing. A lot more wear and tear occurs in transporting the glider than flying it. You can also lose a lot of time rigging a glider that was just stuffed into the bag at the end of the previous day's flying. Try to get an experienced pilot who flies the same make of glider to give you a few tips on the best sequence and where you need protective padding during transportation.

You have to get a feel for the tensions and the pressures needed at each stage of rigging. If it doesn't feel right or requires unusual force . . . STOP. Find out what is wrong. A wire may be snagged, an eye may be twisted . . . Do it again and again until you have got it down to an invariable sequence. This will ensure that you immediately notice if anything is not quite right as you rig and stand you in good stead later when good conditions with others soaring make you want to rush it.

EQUIPMENT

Wind proof clothing is essential for flying or simply standing about on the top of hills. It's more important that the material 'breathes' than that it's waterproof. The initial exertion of carrying up always makes you perspire. Close woven nylon or plastic treated waterproofs trap sweat and become clammy as you cool down. A two part outfit is better than overalls, you can leave the jacket off carrying up and the separate trousers make coping with 'pre-flight accelerated digestion' easier.

Gloves are essential for warmth and protection but also make sure that they improve your grip rather than weaken it. Wear and tear during flying is extremely heavy. Cheap plastic imitation leather will not survive. At least ensure that they have genuine leather on the working surfaces if not on the backs.

Boots. Your feet are the first part to get cold. You need boots that will keep them warm and dry particularly in the winter when sites become wet and boggy. They must also provide you with a sure footing on steep and slippery paths. Types that lace up about 3-4 inches above the ankle are best. They give good support in hard landings on rough ground (don't get the type which take the laces round hooks which can catch a rigging wire when you are flying prone).

Helmets. In the early days it was important to listen to the noises the sail was making and the ears were left uncovered. This is less important with todays well cut sails but you do need to preserve an awareness of the sound of the airstream. Helmets are available made specifically for Hang Gliding with apertures for the ears. I prefer an overall cover to keep them (and the back of my neck) warm but I have removed a section of the lining around the ears so that I can still hear well.

Goggles, Sunglasses are not absolutely essential for every flight. However they do stop your eyes watering badly on cold days and polaroids improve your vision up-sun. On balance I'd say you're wiser to wear a good pair of polaroids. Avoid cheap stained lenses and frames that 'blinker' you.

Wind-speed Indicator. At least one pilot on the hill should have one. It's surprising how the wind-speed varies with your desire to fly when you can't check it accurately.

CHAPTER 6
'GRASSHOPPING'

The club or school will have access to several training sites facing various wind directions. They will consist of a level, unobstructed landing area at the foot of a gently rising and steepening slope. We are going to start near the bottom where the slope is not more than in 1 in 8. Now don't get the idea you are going to fly like a bird (yet). Before you can start, you need to familiarise yourself with the handling. Picking up the glider, holding the attitude, running a few steps, getting a bit 'foot light' and, most important, getting used to slowing and stopping the glider by pushing on the uprights or the control bar to raise the nose and use the wing as an air break. Although the initial pick up is made by putting your head through the control frame and straightening your back. It is easier to support the weight by having one hand on the control bar. The other should be about shoulder high on the upright to give you leverage to raise and lower the nose. Your harness straps should be almost tight. Your instructor will be on the nose wires showing you the correct attitude for your run. (Some 'pitch stable' gliders may allow a both hands on the uprights technique. He will tell you the best method for your glider). After you have practiced this for 10—15 minutes the time has come to try a 'hop' so we move a little higher up the slope. We don't want it so steep that you can't stop running if you get it wrong; 1 - 6 is plenty. The wind will be light and blowing straight up the slope at about 8—10 mph. Any less and you could not run fast enough to attain flying speed. Too much more and you could not experiment without the danger of being blown over backwards. It is also important that the wind is steady, early mornings and evenings are the best times.

You will be able to stand raising and lowering the nose, holding the control frame, so that your harness straps are firm but not tight. Make sure you are pointing directly into wind. (A tell-tale ribbon on the forward wires or a windsock on a stick are well worth having). Adjust the nose so that the wing is just filling and your straps are still firm not tight, you want to be able to feel the lift developing.

All set then . . . Start your run!

You need to reach a speed over the ground (groundspeed) of about 8—10 mph, an olympic sprinter does 20 mph so you won't be breaking records. The wind is blowing the opposite way at 8—10 mph so your speed through the air (airspeed) will be 16—20 mph—enough to get you off the ground for a few yards. If the glider does not immediately start feeling lighter and tightening the harness straps ease the control bar away from you to raise the nose and continue accelerating. If it still shows no sign of lifting you've got the nose too low (and you're probably running out of slope!). Start slowing but keep the nose up. Don't let the glider overfly you and dig its nose in.

If the glider immediately pulls the straps tight when you start your run, tries to snatch you off the ground and needs a lot of pushing, the nose is too high—so slow down, stop and try again.

If your first couple of tentative attempts don't 'come off'—unclip and have a good rest. You will find learning to handle a glider is very hard work, you are using a lot of arm and shoulder muscles that you don't normally call on. Don't keep trying when you're tired. This applies even more if you're a girl. Get as much assistance as you can in the carrying, lifting and steadying. Have people on the cross wires as well as the nose, but remember, once they let go you have to hold it on your own. At the first sign of unsteadiness get the nose down on the ground. Always wear gloves in case your fingers get caught under the control bar when you ground it.

Your instructor will take you through it again and you will probably do another couple of ground runs on the flat. Right, let's go half way up the slope and try again. Your instructor stays down in the landing area to shout instructions. This time you feel more confident. The pick up is better. The nose attitude feels right. The wings are level—you tell the wire man to RELEASE! Pause a moment, check you are dead into wind and start your run. As you steadily accelerate your harness straps tighten—you keep running but in a couple more strides you are running on air.

Almost before you realise this, you are over the flat ground and about to touch down, your brain finally registers that the noise in your ear is a voice shouting PUSH OUT! You do just that! The nose lifts, the glider flares out of it's descent, stalls and deposits you on the ground just slow enough for a few steps to stop from falling over. FANTASTIC! Let's try it again a bit higher.

Not so fast, says your instructor who is concerned that in a flight of more than a few seconds it is very possible for one wing to lift and a turn start to develop. He has to be sure that you can keep the glider straight and level before you attempt any 'BIG HOPS'. In some schools you will have had lessons on turns in their simulator. On the hill you have to think it through and progress a little at a time.

Let's try another short hop. You feel very confident and leaving your instructor in the landing area, you carry up but just a little bit higher. (I knew we were going to have trouble with you). The take off is again good. The ground clearance is a little higher, the speed seems a little faster—TOO FAST! The ground 'arrives' and on touch down you have to run like hell. The glider overflies you, digs its nose in and you pitch forward putting your shoulder into one upright.

Your instructor walks over, studies the bent upright and enquires as to whether you had any particular reason for flying into the ground rather than landing as you have been taught. (Or words to that effect). He does not seem to show a proper concern at your misfortune . . . your shoulder is hurt . . . your pride is hurt and your lovely glider is bent!

Well you're not *dead* and the replacement is only a straight piece of tube (glad it wasn't a more advanced machine?) A school glider would have had wheels fitted to the control bar to reduce this type of accident risk.

Day two is three weeks later because of repairs and conditions not being quite right. This is where schools have all the advantages . . . spare gliders, tethered training, plenty of supervision. As you rig you find yourself checking everything more carefully. After a couple of short hops you realise that you are concentrating harder and planning what you are going to do. That bent upright (and that nasty instructor) did something for you. Somewhere in learning to fly something has to sharpen you up and shift your mind into another 'gear' you didn't know you had. The sooner this happens the better. If it doesn't . . . 'you just ain't gonna make it'.

So now you have to prepare for your first 'big hop' by getting the hang of ROLL CORRECTION, DRIFT and TURNS. If your glider is a modern trainer it will have a keel pocket and will operate as a truly FLEXWING glider. Previously we have talked of turns in purely weight shift terms i.e. using your weight to directly make or offset a change in attitude. Even in a Rogallo, but more so in a true Flexwing, there's more to it than that. Shifting your weight loads one wing more than the other causing that wing to arch along it's trailing edge. On the old standards the sail was fixed to the keel and we spoke of the billow shifting. On the modern glider the keel pocket allows the arching of the loaded sail to tighten the other.

This can be seen from the ground even though it is no more than an inch or two. The effect is quite marked, producing a reduced angle of attack (less lift) on the loaded wing and the opposite effect on the other. The required weight shift is less than on a Rogallo and the response is immediate. We are in fact banking and turning just like a bird does by flexing our wings. Getting the bank off and stopping the turn is just as quick and easy.

What a superb flying machine it is (you are thinking), so simple! so efficient! so let's go up to the top of the slope and see how you feel about this 'big hop'. Standing there it's surprising how much higher the hill has become since the last time you were on top of it. You rig the glider and your pre-flight check somehow takes a lot longer. Your instructor shows you how the wind is not quite straight on. It's coming a little from your right, only about 5°—10°, nothing you can't handle since the crest is smooth, rounded grassland and the windspeed only 12 mph. He points out that once airborne with the wind slightly off to the right, if you keep your nose pointing straight out, you will drift to your left. Not to worry (he says), this will put you to the left of the landing area and allow a gentle right turn to bring you straight into wind for your landing.

Note how a small weight-shift (look at the pilot's elbows) has produced a marked flex. The right trailing edge is arched, the left is pulled much flatter.

A moment of panic—the hill has now increased its height to 1,000 ft—the wind has increased to near gale force—AND—A TURN WILL HAVE TO BE MADE . . . (Please God let me be somewhere else). It's only a moment . . . your training takes over, you know what to do, you check your helmet and harness, check that the sky and landing areas are clear, wings level and nose into wind. Your run is not going to be quite straight down the slope because of the wind direction; but there is nothing to trip you up and the slope drops steeply away. Your instructor impresses on you the importance of gaining airspeed quickly as soon as you are airborne. Speed gives you better control and reduces the risk of stalling. SPEED IS SAFETY.

You check the wind again and line up into it. Wings level, harness straps firm, nose down a little, OK, RELEASE! A shorter run than when you were half way down, three or four strides, you're treading air and pulling speed. The height is a little alarming and you keep the speed on a shade too long. The flight is half over before you ease the bar out and assume the designed flying airspeed.

For the first time you really feel as though you're flying but its only a moment before you realise that you are drifting to the left and that you are going to have to make that turn pretty soon . . . like now!

You pull on speed and weight shift gingerly to your right . . . nothing happens! (Actually you have done little more than tense you muscles and lean your body) . . . you make a more positive sideways movement, really shifting yourself *along* the bar. The glider responds . . . too much . . . you apply opposite correction keeping the speed on . . . she straightens up. The landing area is directly in front of you (surprise). You are dead into wind, not drifting. All you have to do is judge your height and flare at the right moment. Losing height steadily now . . . ground coming up fast . . . too fast! (You're still holding that speed you pulled on for the turn). Ease the bar . . . she levels . . . slows . . . then starts to lose height again. Now it needs a slight push to hold her skimming the ground just a few feet up. She starts to slow and drop again, NOW FLARE! three steps . . . stop . . . make sure you are into wind . . . ground the nose . . . unclip and by a supreme effort of self control, refrain from jumping up and down, waving your arms about and shouting. I know it's difficult because the feeling at the end of that first *real* flight is truly MAGNIFICENT!

Ensuing flights may be spread far apart on different sites. They will be weaving descents of 200—400ft with gentle turns up to ninety degrees and moderate corrective movements. These will all be in winds of 10 to 14mph and virtually straight on. Now is the time for patience, waiting for the right conditions, not taking chances. Have a set sequence for doing everything, even packing your gear and tying your glider on the car. Stick a check list on the inside of the boot lid so you don't forget anything. Don't drive off down the road still arguing with the wife . . . once you set off concentrate on what you are going to do.

CHECKS BEFORE FLYING. Immediately prior to taking off is not the time to be checking for wear and tear on the structural components. This should be done during de-rigging, rigging or, better still, on non-flying days in the back garden.

Rigging Check:- The rigging sequence should be a check in itself both by look and feel, particularly:

Control frame assembly links and wire attachments.

King post seating, top saddle and the upper wires passing through.

Keel and Crosstube links and wire attachments.

Sail stitching and attachment to spars.

Battens and retainers.

Deflexors (if fitted).

Nose wires attachment.

Check the rigged glider for symmetry and if you can get 'clean' wind try to fly it holding the forward wires. Check stability and any tendency to turn.

Pre-Flight Check:- Having studied the conditions and the general flying pattern, you carry forward.

Hook in and check the attachment (if a karibiner, close the gate).

Harness, secure, no twists, seat straps tight (if prone lie in the flying position and get your wire man to check it over).

Helmet fastened and firm.

Other gliders well clear and no obstacles on the ground.

Wind direction and strength, Wings level and not tending to lift or drop one side.

Instruct the wire man to RELEASE . . . and go.

Log every flight however short. Go over what you did wrong (even after your 600th flight). Always make a pre-flight plan to develop and perfect your skills.

TAKING OFF. You will have more than one poor take off. The worst will involve stalling just as you become airborne through letting the nose get too high. You must react *instantly* by pulling on speed and un-

Natalie Wilson, with husband on the wires, gets herself perfectly set before starting her take-off run.

Bob Calvert 'runs right off the hill' in Tennessee, U.S.A., training for the 1980 American Cup. Ramp take-offs are essential in rocky and heavily wooded terrain. The glider is his La Mouette ATLAS (a French fourth generation design) on which he made his 79 mile flight (see Chap. 1).

47

stalling the wing. Until you have achieved this you will not be able to 'pick it up' and stop the turn developing. If you do not react soon enough the wing tip will touch and you will pivot on it into the hill.

Always prepare your take off carefully. Always have an experienced wire man on the nose. Learn to go only when you are perfectly ready (not when others urge you). Be prepared to call it off and let others go if you are not sufficiently confident (you will always feel 'keyed up' but that's not the same thing). Watch the other gliders for a minute or two. See how they are working the lift and judge your clear airspace 'slot' accordingly. Once you have decided to go and have said RELEASE don't dither, provided your wings are level and neither is lifting more than the other, start your run purposefully. It should be a steady acceleration until you 'run right off the hill'. (Keep going as though you were going to run all the way to the bottom).

CONTROL. You will have noticed that we describe most controlling movements in terms of moving the bar rather than 'shifting weight'. As you progress you become increasingly aware that your control capability in good conditions is far more sensitive than the term 'weight shift' suggests. Your suspended weight forms a pendulum with considerable inertia and it is against this that delicate control movements can be made. The actual weight shift is only momentary and quite small. However, as conditions become more difficult due to strong winds, turbulence or thermal activity, corrective movements need to be more generous, truly a matter of shifting your weight about (preferably with great skill and alacrity).

LANDING. Always get your hands on the uprights when you are approaching for a landing. This enables you to push the control frame further from you achieving the fullest possible flare and the lowest possible speed for your touch down. It also keeps your hands out of the way if you stumble and ground the control bar heavily. Don't be afraid to flare a foot or two too high. It is much less likely to cause damage or injury than flying into the ground. In your early landings you may stall much too high once or twice. On a standard Rogallo you need at least 30ft to recover flying speed. If you are below this—DO NOT PULL THE BAR IN (this will result in a dive into the ground). You must stay stalled and 'parachute' in, keep your feet together, knees slightly bent and hold the uprights as far out as you can. The modern trainer will unstall more readily but you still need 20ft to recover. When you pull the bar in be prepared for a rapid loss of height and the need to flare almost immediately.

GROUND EFFECT. Once you are below 10ft, the air being forced downwards by the wing is 'squeezed' between the undersurface and the ground. Additional pressure builds up causing the glider to 'float on' a bit further than you would expect. Be prepared for this and delay your flare accordingly. Prone pilots of high performance gliders can have real problems trying to bring them in on a slight down-slope where ground effect produces a glide angle equal to the angle of the slope itself. If you have a choice, it's always easier to land uphill than downhill.

CHAPTER 7
REACHING PILOT ONE RATING

You really need to get to the big hills over five hundred feet high. These will give you descents of over two minutes duration and the ground clearance necessary to practice steeper turns and stall recovery. It's well worth a trip to the coast to get smoother conditions. You will learn more there in a weekend than in a month on small sites inland. It's always advisable to contact the Coastguards for a report on conditions and a forecast. They will probably quote you windspeeds in terms of the Beaufort Scale.

WIND SCALE	WIND SPEED (in knots)	SEA STATE (abbreviated description)
Force		
0	Less than 1	Sea like a mirror.
1	1—3	Ripples.
2	4—6	Small wavelets, glassy not breaking.
3	7—10	Large wavelets, scattered white horses.
4	11—16	Waves, frequent white horses.
5	17—21	Long waves, many white horses.
6	22—27	Large waves, white foam crests everywhere.
7	28—33	Sea heaps, streaks of foam.
8	34—40	High waves and spindrift. (Gale)

The full scale goes up to Force 12 (Hurricane).

A knot is one nautical mile (approx. 2000 yds). So 14kts is approx. 16 mph. 20kts. is approx. 23 mph. and so on. Bear in mind that the forecast that they give is for the whole sea area and that events may be one or two hours later reaching the coast. A local forecast is sometimes available and always more useful.

A seated pilot pulling the bar into his stomach and sticking his legs and head forward will not be able to sustain an airspeed much above 25mph. Any wind over force 4 (11—16 kts at sea level) will be over 23 mph on the crest of the ridge. If he makes his take off with a low airspeed he will not penetrate out. He will find himself pointing forwards, desperately trying to pull on more speed, but actually going steadily backwards. A landing from this situation is always painful and expensive. The best course of action depends on the site but as a general rule it's better to gain height and land well back rather than immediately behind the crest where there is probably some rotor effect.

On no account go to a cliff site. You want a coastal ridge about 1 in 3 to 1 in 4 slope with a good unobstructed beach landing. A couple of days there and you can do the rest inland.

Contact the Local Club, find out the site rules and send any site fee (if required). On arrival find a Club Officer or an Observer (badge says Observer; he will also be rated Pilot two). Tell them who you are and what experience you've got. They will give you an assessment of conditions and advise you if it's O.K. for you to fly. Don't be in any sort of a hurry, spend at least a quarter of an hour watching the locals.

If the wind is very light just rig and wait. You don't want to try anything approaching a nil wind take off for your first flight. Let's say you're lucky and it's about 10—12 mph straight on. A local 'super ace' in a 'super ship' is miraculously soaring to and fro in front of the take off area (have faith your time will come). Select a couple of experieced pilots and chat them up. They are not officials but because of the traumatic history of site negotiations in Hang Gliding the initial conversation goes something like this. (First the Gestapo bit) Who are you? What club? How long have you been flying? Where? ('Ve haf vays of making you talk'). Then the Site Rules bit. Don't overfly the caravans, don't land in the bottom fields, keep away from the cliffs . . . after which they seem to expect you to soar. 'The lift is quite good if you stick in close where John (Super Ace) is now. . ."Don't try to jump the gully until you have about a hundred feet' . . . from which you gather that you have been accepted and they will help you to take off.

You'll feel a bit 'keyed up (strange site, higher ridge) but do your usual pre-flight check, methodically make your pre-flight plan and pick your approx. landing spot even though there are two square miles of beach available. Make it fairly well out in clean wind if you can. Not close in at the foot of the slope. Try to assess if the lower wind is tending to 'funnel' *along* the beach and plan your approach into it.

Usual last checks . . . other gliders clear . . . wings level . . . RELEASE . . . three or four strides, you're off the crest, airborne and pulling on a touch of speed. You look down. TERROR in the shape of six hundred feet ground clearance hits you right in the guts! (Please God just let me get down . . .). You're soon through the 'lift band' and beginning to descend. Time for your first turn to travel along the ridge. You pull on just a 'midge' of speed and weight shift for a gentle bank . . . nicely, speed building . . . push a little on the bar to stop the nose dropping any more . . . not too much . . . centralise weight to keep the bank constant . . . almost parallel with the ridge . . . pull a little speed and rrrrrooll her out.

WOOSH! . . . a soaring glider passes overhead only just clearing the top rigging! (by thirty feet actually). The prone 'ace' under it smiles and waves . . . you give a sickly grin back, keeping both hands firmly on the bar.

Who didn't see the other glider then? Who didn't have a good look round before he turned? . . . B.H.G.A. Flying Rule No. 1: Never remain looking in one direction for more than two or three seconds; always be aware of the position and movement of other gliders.

More aware that you are no longer ground hopping, but sharing a ridge with others, you keep 'rubber necking' as you make your turn out towards the beach. Thoroughly enjoying yourself now aren't you, feeling a bit sorry it's going to be over soon, thinking you could have stayed in a bit closer, held the lift a bit longer, not lost so much in the turns . . . Welcome to the club!

It's a bit tricky judging your height over a flat featureless beach but once you're really low it's easier and you make just about your best touch down yet. The long climb back up takes half an hour. (A girl might take a good deal longer without help. But, you see them doing it! They're a tough lot are our 'Ladybirds').

Take it easy. Don't be in too much of a hurry to get another flight in. Savour the moment and take a good look at the conditions; they are never quite the same. Never fly anywhere by habit. *Always fly the conditions, not the ridge.* Slight changes in wind strength and direction can make a lot of difference.

This time you should try a stall and recovery.

'You must be joking'.

Did I hear right? What happened to that troublesome adventurous character you used to be in earlier chapters?

Sure enough the wind has gone round, a shade more south in it now. But up the north end there's a spur jutting out that will give a straight run into wind. (Fig. 14). It's increased slightly to 14—16 mph. and everyone else is soaring. Nobody to take the wires.

The minutes drag on, you think about an unassisted take off. Not here, not yet, be patient, don't take chances. At last somebody top lands and is only too pleased to help you. "Turn south straight away (he says) you can get a couple of hundred feet before you get to the gulley, by the time you get back this end to round the spur you'll have so much height you won't know it's there . . ." (he says).

You are concentrating on picking a good spot for your take off. The ground is a lot rougher on the spur. When you are all set and get him to raise the nose you feel the glider is damn near taking itself off. The wind has picked up even more. (good job you did't try that unassisted take off). A good look round and your helper suggests you go forward of the crest and down the face a few yards. Good thinking, you agree, because you are not going to make any sort of run in this strength of wind.

The other gliders are well above. It's a bit difficult keeping the wings level . . . the right one keep lifting. your wire man is having to pull down hard and is looking a little anxious. . . He knows you're not getting it right and tells you so. You realise what's wrong and together you get the nose lower until the wing is 'neutral'. That feels better, you have control and can keep it level (never take off when your wire man is having to pull down hard) . . . last check for other gliders . . . RELEASE . . . One step forward. Your foot doesn't touch the ground, you're climbing away and pulling on speed. That was just about the easiest take off you have ever done. (It was actually stronger than you thought, more like 18 mph. Your helper was an experienced pilot and knew how to look after a

beginner. Glad you waited for him?) You are worried
by the wind strength and anxious to get well away
from the ridge. At position A (Fig. 14) you are
surprised to have only lost 60ft after turning to track
along the ridge. (Your track is your path over the
ground which can be quite different to your heading
i.e. the direction in which your nose is pointing). Your
groundspeed seems quite slow with the wind off to the
south. (A lot slower than on your last flight but it
doesn't really register how much as you fly from A. to
B.)

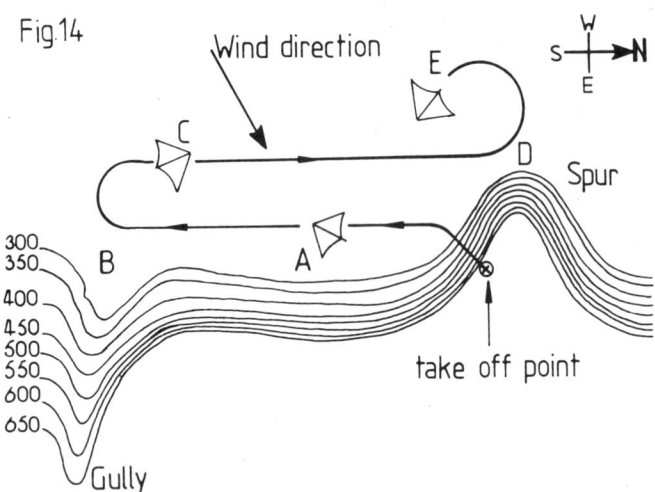

Fig.14

Wind direction

At position B the ridge is less steep and is cut by a
gulley. You find yourself losing height. You decide on a
steepish turn so as not to get too much further out but
you don't get the speed and bank well co-ordinated.
Damn (you're thinking) another 50ft gone . . . too far
out and going down . . . *again*. From positions C to D
you are really covering the ground fast and still losing
height (something should be warning you) . . .
Determined not to throw any more height away you
decide to make the next turn 'flatter', not too steeply
banked. You intend to turn short of the spur, in the

best lift, but your speed over the ground surprises you and you overshoot.

Opposite the spur you go into the turn gently trying to make it 'flat' while looking over your shoulder. The left wing drops sharply as you start to bank. You opposite-weight-shift to pick it up. The glider feels as though it's on the rails ... TOTALLY UNRESPONSIVE ... You are now at position E. steeply banked and heading straight for the ridge ... All your instincts for self-preservation are willing you to push out, slow down for the impact, try to turn away ... Your training says PULL SPEED—REGAIN CONTROL. You do! Immediately the glider seems to come 'unstuck' and you make a diving right hand turn towards the beach ... PHEW! ... what happened then?

You have just experienced an incipient stall in a turn.

Let's go back to that slow groundspeed from A to B. You were dropping a little below the crest and it should have warned you that lower down the wind was beginning to 'funnel' more *along* the ridge than at the top. Lower still from C to D you were practically flying *downwind* especially opposite the spur (cliffs and spurs always increase funneling effects). You didn't read the situation well enough and looking down between C and D you allowed your *high groundspeed* to mislead you into letting your *airspeed* drop. It was already dangerously near the stall when you went into your left turn *without increasing your airspeed*. As the left wing went down it began to stall where it's angle of attack was highest near the centre. Your opposite weight shift correction only made things worse by increasing the angle of attack of the wing that was already stalling. (Fig. 15)

The loss of lift and *increasing drag* steepened and increased the rate of turn. Fortunately your training took over otherwise you would not have been the first (or the last) to finish up in hospital through making this mistake.

Towards late afternoon the wind veers (moves clockwise looking from above; if it swung the other

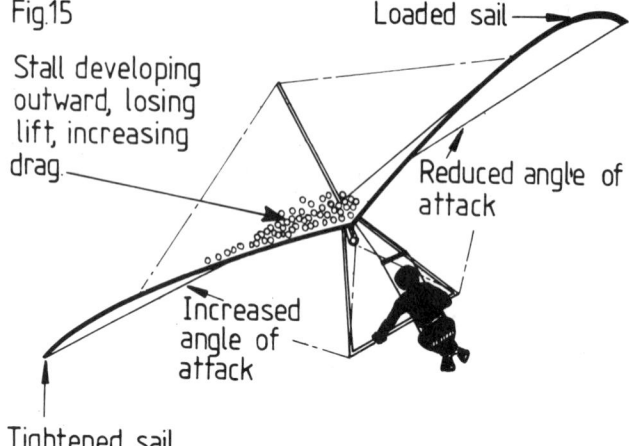

Fig.15

Loaded sail

Stall developing outward, losing lift, increasing drag.

Reduced angle of attack

Increased angle of attack

Tightened sail

way we would say it backed. These are old sailing terms but still in use). It's now straight on but dropping gradually all the time. You get two more flights in, the first your longest yet, 3 mins 45½ secs. including a tentative stall and recovery (on purpose this time). Some kids draw a big square in the sand and scrawl HEATHROW underneath. You reckon you land your '707' plumb centre of Slough but they all cheer and help you carry it back up the beach.

Relaxing in the pub reflecting on the days events, you never felt quite so alive and a pint never tasted quite so good.

You're thinking . . . there didn't seem a lot to the stall, plenty of height, straight into wind, pushing the bar out further . . . suddenly the nose drops, the left wing too, pull on speed, pick up the wing, level out, nothing to it . . . much! . . . Wonder what actually happened in that bad turn. Turbulence? Too slow? . . . got to talk it over with the others. You sit listening to the club experts discussing . . . 1200ft above the beach, . . . 'multiple three sixties', . . . 'chandelles' (whatever they are) . . . you pluck up courage and ask about your near accident. Glasses are positioned, lines are drawn in spilt beer, at least three 'ace' pilots are talking to you . . . THIS IS LIVIN'.

Your next day out is back on the old inland lower ridge. It's varying 12—18 mph. Occasionally down to 10. It's also well off about 15—20 degrees. The first flight is a near disaster, you don't get your run quite into wind, a wing drops and by the time you pick it up you're half way down. It's as bumpy as hell. You manage a couple of fairly fast turns and at least get it down on the dry patch to de-rig. You don't need me to tell you that you were in too much of a hurry, too keen to get into the air and didn't spend enough time weighing up the conditions . . . you spend the whole climb back up telling yourself that. (I wonder what happened to all that fear we used to worry about).

Later on it drops and steadies to 10—14 mph. It's more or less straight on, so how about trying an un-assisted take off. This means a change of technique. Go back well behind the take off area. Have a wire man to begin with and try a few practice walks. You need to use your shoulders to exert forward pressure. Using a 'pint holding grip' on both uprights lift the control frame until the uprights sit firmly against each shoulder (harness straps will be slack). Practise raising and lowering the nose as you walk into wind, keeping your wire man ready to grab them if the nose lifts too much. (see photograph on page 58).

Practise this for about ten minutes until you really feel you've got it sorted out. Right then . . . all checks completed . . . take up a position a few yards back. No trouble keeping the nose position right, push with the shoulders, pull with the hands. Check for other gliders (not so easy, the sail is lower and you can't see so much. Get another *pilot* to check for you). Into wind and wings level, nobody to say release to . . . so go . . . Push with the shoulders and start your run, don't grip too tightly on the uprights (a stumble could give you a badly sprained wrist). Two or three strides and she starts to lift. As your hands come level with your shoulders, drop one onto the bar and keep accelerating. Two more strides and the straps tighten as you reach the edge. You have flying speed and are airborne in the next stride. Drop the other hand onto the bar, pull on a little speed and turn along the ridge:

You're still at take off height when you get to your

The unassisted take-off position.

turn out; this is better. Not much lost in the turn but it took you too far out and the lift band is not so wide the wind has dropped. At the other end a bit of turbulence demands a faster turn and you're half way down ... Lost it again. Never mind it won't be worth carrying up again so let's make this a perfect 'spot landing' right by the track. Its nicely judged and you're down like a feather.

You have now done everything required for Pilot One rating. A school might have got you through it all in two or three weekends and issued your certificate. The club learner needs to demonstrate each task to a Club Official, Observer or qualified Instructor. It is quite incredible how, if you land in an unauthorised field, Observers and Club Officials emerge from under every cow-pat! Just try to find one when you want to demonstrate your competence. They are as rare as thermals at weekends!

Summer goes, the weather deteriorates and winds are perverse. This is the most difficult period of learning when you have become more confident and are often tempted to fly in conditions beyond your skill. Remember the old flying saying...

'There are *old* pilots and there are *bold* pilots but there are *no old bold* pilots'.

CHAPTER 8
RIDGE SOARING

To mark your glorious attainment at getting rated Pilot One we will now change the character of the text to one of flying together rather than lecturing you. Actually all pilots talk to themselves when they are flying so you might as well get used to it. Shall *we* continue . . .

First we need a better understanding of glider performance. Fig. 6 showed our total drag to be lowest (40lbs) at an airspeed of 20—21 mph. Since the lift produced in straight flight must equal the total weight (240lbs) our ratio of lift to drag is 6 to 1. If we fly faster or slower total drag increases and our Lift to Drag

Ratio reduces. We say 20—21 mph is our 'Best L/D'.

To overcome drag we have to descend at a glide angle equal and opposite to our L/D ratio. In one minute of flight at 20—21 mph we will travel approx. 1800ft and descend 300ft (in still air). This is our 'Best Glide Angle' (1800 to 300 = 6 to 1). However, if we fly at 18 to 19 mph total drag only increased to 43lbs. Although our Glide Angle is steeper, 5. 6 to 1, we are flying slower and in one minute travel approx. 1600ft and descend 285ft. We haven't travelled as far but we haven't lost as much height. We say 18—19 mph is our 'Min Sink' (Minimum Sink). These relationships vary slightly from glider to glider but in general Min Sink is about 2 mph slower than Best L/D.

As long as the air passing over a ridge is being forced to rise faster than our rate of descent, we can soar.

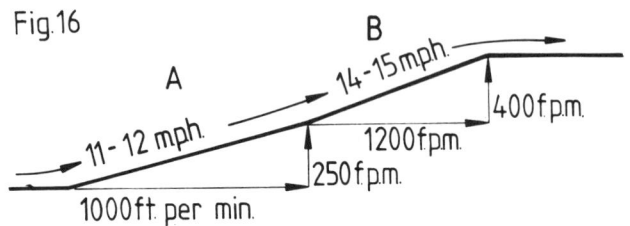

Fig.16

In section A the slope is 1 in 4 and the wind 11—12 mph. This can be resolved as a horizontal component of 1000ft per min. and a vertical component of 250ft per min. Our rate of descent is 285—300ft per min. This is greater than the vertical component so we cannot stay up. In section B the slope is 1 in 3 and the wind speed increased to 14—15 mph. The horizontal component is 1200ft per min. and the vertical component is 400ft per min. Our rate of descent is less than the vertical component so *we can not only stay up but actually gain altitude.*

Unfortunately, as we fly along the ridge neither the speed of the wind nor the angle of the slope remain constant. Pilots talk of the lift being good or the sink being bad or the turbulence being evil. It is a more colourful and understandable way of describing rapid variations in the vertical component.

HOW DO WE STOP GOING DOWN? Obviously first soaring flights are far more a matter of good conditions on good sites rather than greatly developed skill. Let's face it, in a 25 mph wind up a 1 in 2 slope even a brick could fly. The first major hurdle to overcome is fear of being too close to the ridge. Up to now, lack of experience has required a rapid increase in airspeed from take off, giving plenty of ground clearance to allow for a mistake. This took you through and out of the best lift area. All this has to change.

Airspeed has to be adjusted to 'Best L/D' within a second or two after take off (the glider is trimmed for it). We don't use 'min sink', it would put us too near our stalling speed. The turn to track along the ridge must start within 50—60ft and must be held on (as must all subsequent turns) until we are closing back towards the ridge, *not getting further out.*

Take a good look at Figs. 11 and 13 again. In the compressed and accelerated 'lift band' the effects of turbulence are reduced and we are actually going to find it easier to fly there than further out. Since the lift is better we can afford to fly faster without losing height. The extra speed gives us quicker response and better control. We have to stay close!

HOW CLOSE IS CLOSE! The limit of how close we can fly is determined by the character of the wind gradient. This is less critical in wind speeds below 10 mph but since these would not be soarable conditions for us as yet, they need not feature in this chapter. We are also less concerned about winds over 18 mph when the lift will extend well out and any turbulence will be strong. We would not need, *or choose*, to fly close to the ridge in these conditions. Our concern is with winds between 10 and 18 mph.

On high smooth unbroken ridge faces you can fly as close as 60ft above or in front of the crest where the wind gradient is compressed. However, if the ridge is interspersed with gullies and outcrops, 120ft is your minimum distance from ground to nearest part of the glider. When this close never let your speed drop below 'best L/D'. You need quick response to inputs .. Speed is safety!

Ledges, shelves, buttresses, walls, trees etc. etc. all produce turbulence. The less steep the slope, the less the wind gradient is compressed and the more noticeable are their effects. As we move down from the crest the wind gradient extends further out. Where all these effects combine conditions can be really 'evil'. Fig. 17 is a simplified illustration of the sort of thing that can happen.

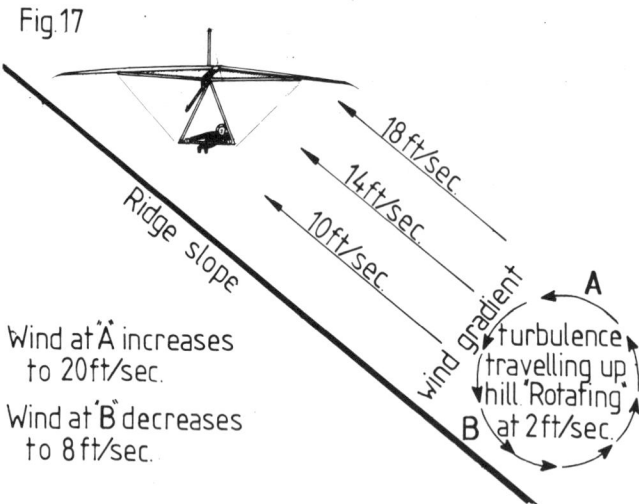

Fig.17

Ridge slope

18ft/sec.

14ft/sec.

10ft/sec.

wind gradient

A

turbulence
(travelling up
hill 'Rotating'
at 2ft/sec.

B

Wind at 'A' increases
to 20ft/sec.

Wind at 'B' decreases
to 8ft/sec.

The wind gradient is already producing a 4—6 degree greater angle of attack on the outside wing which the pilot is offsetting by shifting his weight to stay level. It needs only a small ground feature causing a swirl of turbulence for the situation to be suddenly intensified. The inside wing meets a momentary lull and loses lift. It drops and may even stall. The outside wing meets a momentary gust and lifts. The pilot is already using half his total corrective cabability to stay level. What he has left will not be enough to cope with the suddeness or strength of the change and he will be turned into the hill. 'Scratching' along at low speed, half way down in these conditions, is asking for trouble.

We'll assume that we can't get to a big coastal site and make it easier for ourselves. Let's say the best we have is an inland ridge about 500ft high with about 200 yds of fairly unbroken 1 in 4 slope, steepening a little more near the top. At this stage we need a wind of at least 16 mph blowing virtually straight on, to give us a soaring flight.

Lets look at the problems one at a time . . .

1. Other gliders, how many? Is there a pattern? We can't hope to succeed if we have to 'mix it'. So we have to be patient or if numbers are small and they are all fellow club members, they might be persuaded to watch the momentous event *from the ground* (well . . . its worth a try anyway).

2. The wind is never absolutely dead straight on. The lift always seems slightly better one way i.e. less ground covered for every foot of height gained. (Oh yes, we are going to go up! THINK UP!) This dictates which way we are going to turn from take off.

3. We choose the end which gives us the longest first beat into the best lift. We don't take off in the middle.

4. The take off will take us out a bit, so our first turn to track along the ridge will have to be kept going until we are closing towards the ridge, not getting further out.

5. We must know the four basic flying rules. These were set out by the B.H.G.A. and embody air law.

No. 1 Look round ... (you already know from Chapter 7).

No. 2 In an imminent head on collision situation, alter course to your right.

No. 3 Give way to gliders a) On your right
                        b) That are turning
                        c) That are below you.

No. 4 Keep 100ft apart. When converging from any direction slow your closing speed and turn away.

Let's not try too much, see what can be made of the

first two beats and if we still have height maybe we can repeat the pattern. The wind is slightly off to the north so we take off at the south end (Fig. 18). It's about 18mph on the crest. We need a wire man. The other gliders are way above so we don't need any favours. Checks complete, we go forward just down the front a yard or two, nose angle low, wire man just steadying a neutral wing not pulling down hard. Into wind, wings level, all clear—RELEASE.

Two steps and we're airborne, just pulling the merest touch of extra speed. We are very used to the bar positions now, hard in, legs forward is about 26—28 mph, half in 22—24 mph, no pressure (or neutral) 20—21 mph, slight push 18—19 mph, firm push but not full stretch 17—18 mph, any more and we stall!

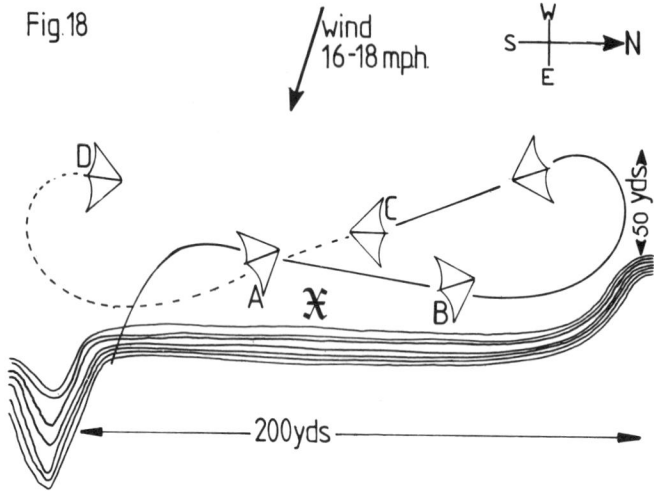

Fig. 18

wind
16-18 mph.

200yds

50 yds

We hold the touch of speed making our first turn without adding to it and keep her coming round till we are just beginning to close back in. At position A we start to ease the nose out and make our track about 30—40 yds out. It seems to point more *along* than one would expect. Bear in mind the wind is angled *up* the face and has a *large vertical component.* The *horizontal component* we are countering is probably only 13 mph.

Never mind the theory, use our eyes and close in a bit more. This is happening anyway as the ridge 'comes out' to meet us at B. We let this go on so that by starting our turn close in, we won't be too far out when we complete it . . . we are climbing, and seem to have gained 100ft (50ft actually) as the end of the beat approaches. A good look around . . . we have clear airspace . . . pull on speed and roll her in . . . bank a bit steeper to keep it tight but we don't push the bar forward enough to stop the nose dropping. Damn! . . . roll her out. No, not yet. Keep her coming round a bit more, we've lost height so we must get back in. Keep the turn on, get back in, *get back in,* GET BACK IN.

Heading south towards the centre of the beat we start climbing again; the keel is about parallel with the ridge at C and we are steadily 'crabbing' in. We are flying at best L/D., we've been airborne about a minute and are back level with take off height. Keep closing so that we are no more than 20—30 yds out when we start our turn. Groundspeed is a bit higher on this leg and we overshoot the turning point, we turn in front of the gulley, the wind is stronger and the lift is less (less vertical component). This turn is better, but we still lose 30ft. Keep it coming round, we've got to get back into that lift band. The ridge comes into view at D ... HELL, THERE'S ANOTHER GLIDER RIGHT WHERE WE WANT TO GO! Right in the middle of the beat at X. Some Ace has overshot his top landing and is 'Hogging it' to regain height and go round again.

We have about 3 seconds to make up our minds what we are going to do. In two seconds we've decided to stay well out and well clear. We have lost another 50' and are too wary of closing in well below the crest. Alas, we're out of 'lift' and going down. The descent is filled with a profound sadness.

What would an experienced pilot have done? Firstly, he would have been aware that the other glider had gone in for a top landing. In his own turn he would have been looking round more, seen it overshoot, rolled out of his own turn and 'sat', (held his position into the wind hovering over one spot) for a moment or two, to see which way the other glider was going to turn. If it made a right turn, he would slot in behind and below (avoiding the other glider's 'wash'). If it made a left turn in behind him, he would pick up his own pattern again. The ability to hold your position and 'sit' over one spot is essential to 'mixing it' in crowded airspace. Sometimes the pattern of several gliders soaring gets upset and the less pilots are throwing their gliders all over the sky the better.

In light winds below our stalling speed it is impossible to remain over one spot. These would be described as MARGINAL CONDITIONS and on some difficult sites (cliffs and the like) numbers in the air would be deliberately restricted. A very definate pattern of soaring would be established. This usually means staying in close on the upwind (slow groundspeed) leg and flying 'outside' on the downwind (fast groundspeed) leg. Always study the pattern that has been established and try to fit in with it. There's nothing worse (and you will see them) than some 'clown' showing off and flying in a totally unpredictable manner.

Back up and ready to go again, the wind is stronger,

Fig.19

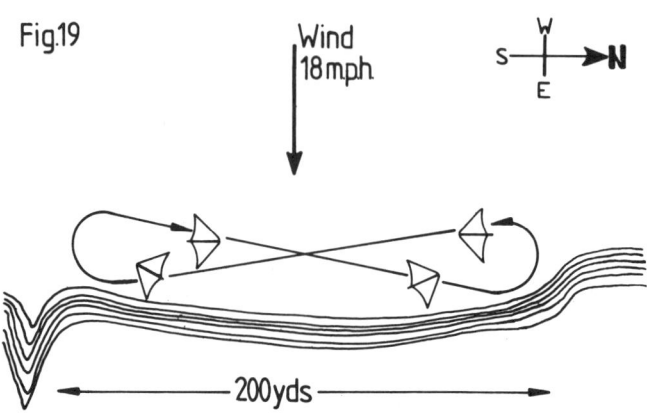

Wind 18 mph

S—W—N E

←——— 200 yds ———→

over, 20 mph at times. At the end of the first beat we have gained 100ft (genuine). Turning is quicker and we are not getting half as far out. (In higher windspeeds turns can become almost a pivot above a particular spot of ground). On the second beat there is less need to make a marked effort to close in because we haven't got all that far out. As we arrive back opposite take off we are 150ft above the crest. Now we can establish a tidy figure-of-eight pattern and start weighing up where the best lift is.

For the first time we really get our airspeed down to 'min sink' (higher in the turns). The experts are well above so we have this level to ourselves and WE ARE SOARING . . . for the very first time we gaze *down* at white *upturned* faces in the take off area. After ten minutes delusions of grandeur set in . . . what are those tiny ant like creatures down there? Can they be intelligent? . . . Enough of that, days like this are too few and far between to squander. We still have a lot to learn. Let's try closing in above the crest and even behind it a yard or two. It's well rounded, the lift will extend well back (30—40 yds) and we have plenty of height. We try it . . . nothing to it.

Tighter turns need practice. We pull on speed, almost excessively, roll into a steeper bank and push firmly to keep the nose coming round parallel with the horizon and not dropping. We need to experiment to get the co-ordination right so we make sure we have plenty of height, clear airspace and higher than normal airspeed each time. Bear in mind the acceleration of the turn increases our wing loading and our stalling speed increases.

Angle of bank (degrees).	Airspeed at the stall
0	16 mph
20	17 mph
30	18 mph
40	19 mph
50	20 mph
60	22 mph

*. . . for the very first time we gaze **down** at white **upturned** faces in the take-off area . . .*

A heavier pilot flying this same glider would stall at higher airspeeds. Figures also vary from glider to glider but the principle stays the same.

Back to the flight . . . we have been airborne for 30 minutes! But another glider has taken off and is staying at our level. He seems to be flying a lot slower than we are and it's making it ten times more diffcult to maintain our pattern. It's getting harder and harder to regain any height we lose, legs and arms are aching . . . time to call it a day. There are a couple of beginners de-rigging at the bottom; let's see how close we can get to them for a spot landing. We drop in lightly about 20 yds away and are addressed with suitable respect. Shall we tell them it was our first soaring flight? We shall not!

There will now follow an unprecedented period of gales, adverse winds, low cloud, rain and fog. We will need all the discretion we can find to avoid doing something stupid. We can handle winds up to 20 mph provided they are more or less straight on but we will have to settle for a few more 'top to bottoms' before our next soaring flight. During this time the opportunity to attempt a couple of nil-wind take offs is bound to present itself.

NIL-WIND TAKE OFFS. Don't attempt them on anything other than good smooth ground where there is at least 8—10 yds to build up speed without any danger of tripping. The slope must drop away steeply so we can gain airspeed with no danger of touching the ground again. It is not possible to run fast enough to attain *full* flying speed but we can get very close to it.

"Isn't it a bit risky?"

"Too right it is, if you get it wrong."

Whether you hold the control bar or the uprights you must pull the harness straps up tight before you start your run. This transfers the thrust from your shoulders to a high point on the glider while your hands control the nose angle. Our aim is a smooth steady acceleration reaching our maximum speed at the point where the hill drops away and we become airborne. We start about 8—10 yds back; it needs resolve determination and a complete commitment. After two or three paces we feel lift being developed but not enough to make us 'foot light'. Keep going hard, don't jerk or try to jump into the air. As the hill drops away we become airborne with the bar slightly back from its normal flying position. It is only a second or two before she picks up full flying speed and we can ease the bar and swoop away.

Andrew Hill, straps tight, prepares for a nil-wind take off at Mill Hill. He obtained his Wings at 16 years of age, finished 28th in the National League a year later.

. . . It needs resolve, determination and a complete commitment. . .

71

There is very little need to do nil-wind take offs. Perhaps at the end of a frustrating day when there has been no wind you will want to fly it down to the car park rather than carry it. You probably feel a bit fed up and stiff from standing about, particularly if you are not so young. Do a bit of a loosening up and get the circulation going before you attempt it and don't go if there is the slightest TAIL WIND.

TOP LANDING is fundamental to really getting into regular soaring. For our first attempt we need a good site. We avoid anywhere where the crest is sharp and the ground falls away behind. This will produce a ROTOR effect and it will not be possible to top land there. Other sites may have trees, buildings, walls or parked cars restricting the top landing area. We want a rounded crest with at least 100 yds of horizontal or only very slightly rising ground behind. It also does wonders for our confidence if a fellow pilot positions himself there to grab our wires on touch down.

Just for once conditions are perfect when we arrive (It does happen sometimes). Wind 18—20 mph about 15° off to the North. After 10 mins we've 'topped out' at about 300ft above the ridge and are making a neat soaring pattern with two other gliders. The only

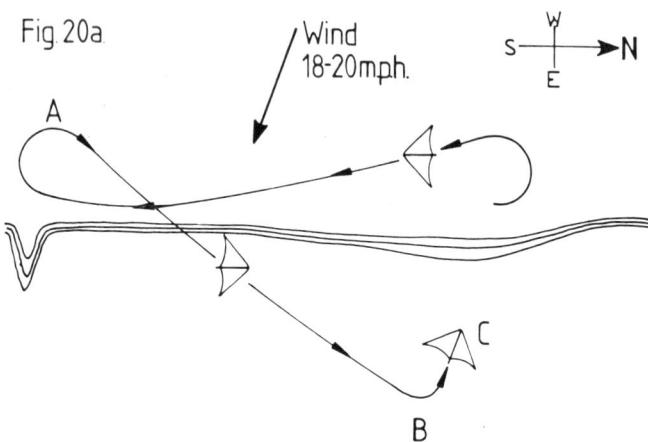

Fig. 20a

Wind
18-20mph.

A

B

C

problem we've had is that occasionally one of them passes in the opposite direction in front and below us so that we have to fly through the 'wash'. The bump is a bit disconcerting (the first time) but we soon get used to anticipating it, pulling on a little speed and ploughing through it. The point is, we've got it sorted' and can concentrate on landing. We only need to keep half an eye on the other two. We've seen one or two others top land so we've a fair idea of what we are going to do. We want to settle our nerves and make it a carefully weighed up cool and methodical manoeuvre. Our groundspeed will be slower going north. All we are going to do is track over the crest from A to B (Fig. 20), turn into wind and touch down at C.

Fig. 20b.

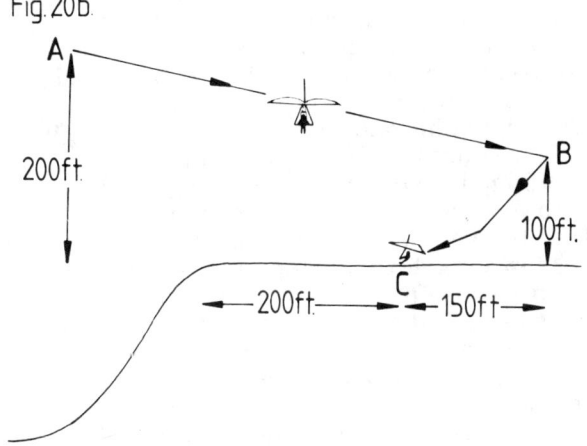

Going in on the slower groundspeed leg gives us more time to weigh things up, an easier chance to turn out and overshoot and less danger of a downwind stall. We need 150—200ft in hand at point A to reach point B. Once behind the crest we shall begin to lose height steadily and will experience some turbulence. Half way from A to B we are committed and will not be able to turn out and overshoot. Height is no longer of advantage so we keep our airspeed a little high for better control. We must go well back so that our touch down is at least 50 yds behind the crest (when we get better at it, all these distances will reduce). Our final turn into wind should put us 75—100ft above and 100—150ft behind our chosen spot. The stronger the wind the lower and nearer we should aim to be.

Let's pick up our flight again on the downwind south-going leg. When we reach point A our height is inadequate (we always seem to lose a bit on the downwind leg). Going north we get in close and really work at gaining height. (Never be in too much of a hurry to get down. It's always worth another couple of beats to get it right). Back at A we've got our 150—200ft and keep the turn going until we are tracking 'crabwise' over the crest. It gets bumpy and we concentrate on keeping extra speed on and the wings level. We don't let the slightest suggestion of an inadvertent turn develop. Losing height steadily, but not as fast as we expected, we pick our spot and turn into wind, finding ourselves a shade too high. The first part of the descent is quite steep (airspeed 22 mph wind 18 mph). We seem to be taking a hell of a long time to get down. Our rate of descent varies. Gusts and lulls in the wind are felt as 'checks' and 'drops' like going down in a lift that stops at one or two floors on the way. At one point we actually start going back up for a moment. It's turbulent alright, first one wing being lifted and then the other. We concentrate and work hard at keeping them level. It's absolutely vital that we *control the descent*. We don't just let it happen. There's no point in delay so we pull on speed and get her down. Only slow if we are penetrating too much and look like overshooting (this won't happen in this wind strength).

In the last 50ft or so we suddenly feel the affect of the wind gradient. As we drop into slower moving air our rate of descent and groundspeed increase rapidly. Had we been flying slowly at a high angle of attack we could have experienced a sudden drop, producing an unintentional stall. The subsequent contact with the ground would have been both painful and expensive.

As it is, we have enough angle of attack in hand to check the increased rate of descent and touch down firmly going forward. We do not flare in the full sense of the word. Once down we keep the sail neutral, step through the control frame and hold the forward wires. It's very nice if help arrives at this point but if it doesn't then unclip from this position. (Whatever else you do make sure the wind does not get under the nose and lift it or you will certainly 'ground loop' i.e. get blown over backwards.)

Just flex the legs, have a cup of coffee and in five minutes we can take off again. We spend the rest of the day doing as many top landings as we can. By late afternoon we've decided they are easier than bottom landings and have decided that we are never 'going down' again.

GOING PRONE. It's time to be thinking about converting to the prone flying position. Why convert? Primarily to reduce form drag, increase our speed range and improve our overall control capability. The ability to pull ourselves through the control frame and fly much faster, will enable us to handle stronger winds. There is also the (deplorable) fact that it looks more stylish and feeds our ego!

We can also start thinking of a higher-performance Intermediate glider (which may well be designed for prone control only). Which step you take first depends on how easily your present glider converts. The rigging system must have a built-in facility for moving the control bar to a further forward position. We also need to buy a prone harness that can be adjusted to the correct height for the control frame. If we can do this, it's easier to convert on the glider that we are used to.

However there are a number of Intermediate gliders designed to convert easily. If you choose this option don't be in too much of a hurry to go prone. Fly seated until you are thoroughly familiar with the handling. You are at the most vulnerable stage in your flying career. More bad mistakes are made by pilots attempting too many changes all at once. We have a saying 'only one first at a time' (the OOFAAT principle). Make your changes one by one. Don't go to a *new site* with a *new glider* and *convert to prone*—you will be committing suicide. It's happened more than twice!

Let's say we go for option two and buy an Intermediate glider that is designed to convert to prone. Above all, we chose one that handles easily and does not demand any marked changes in technique to fly it. The object of the exercise is to *go prone and then learn how to fly a wider range of conditions.* We'll get some excellent soaring in and maybe a couple of cross country flights as well, but it will be twelve months before we're ready for the 'fantastic thermal hookin', cloud bustin', oxygen-equipped FABULOSTRATOS 2000 XC from Britain's leading manufacturer' (whoever that happens to be at the time).

There may be a prone harness on offer with the glider and it may suit you. If not, try as many as you can. This is where the big annual events are useful; the manufacturers are all there and you can shop around.

Having picked one that suits your physique and weight, rig a hook somewhere that you can suspend yourself on and 'rotate' from seated to prone without your feet touching the ground. You will need something firm to push on (I used an old washing machine) to simulate the control bar. Practise, practise, practise, rotating, picking up the stirrup, moving laterally, forwards and backwards. Spend at least half an hour in the harness each session getting your neck and shoulder muscles accustomed to new demands.

Get plenty of seated-flying in on the new glider. Taking off will be easier, the better lift characteristics will not demand quite so much effort. You will be surprised by the quicker response to control movements and you will find yourself over-correcting for a while. The height gains will seem incredible. You will only need a couple of hours soaring to become thoroughly familiar with the new machine. Don't waste time just 'swanning' about, practice steep turns, steeper turns, stalls, recovering and top landings. try a

360 or two. There is no mystery about them (It's only 2 x 180's put together). Don't 'lock' into them. Make them big and fly it all the way round. In a gentle 360 with only 10—15 degrees of bank, most well-designed gliders will virtually fly themselves round in about a 200ft diameter circle. Just make sure you have plenty of height and clear airspace behind you. Always have an extra special look round before committing yourself. Steep multiple 360's are different; you are not ready for them yet.

At last the great day arrives on which you can go prone. Perfect soaring conditions on one of your best sites. You do a couple of seated flights first to 'suss' things out. Take your time altering the rigging for prone flight, make sure it is done correctly. It may not be simply a matter of changing the bar position, you may have to alter the attachment position on the upright as well. (When all else fails read the instructions). It is vital to get your harness adjusted exactly right and to the correct height. You must have an experienced pilot to help you (friends will not do). Preferably, one who flies with the same type of harness.

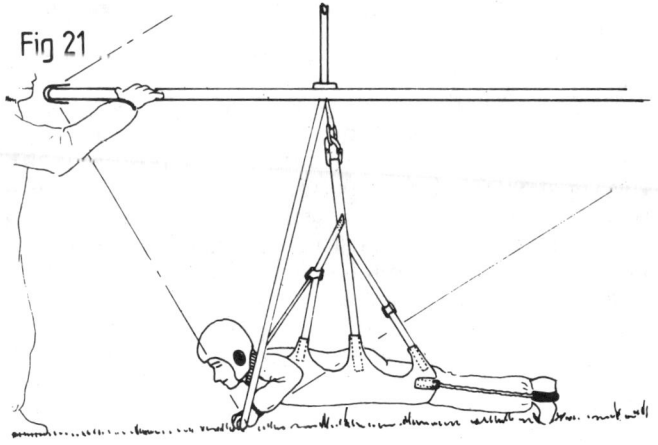

Fig 21

Lying in the flying position, get your nose man to raise and lower the nose. As you swing through you should just be able to pass your gloved hand (palm facing your toes) between your harness and the control bar. I prefer to use a safety loop made from strong elastic or shock cord to keep the stirrup under control so that I can get my free foot in without looking or groping for it. Secure it slightly off-centre, *then tape it so it doesn't slip.*

Fig. 22

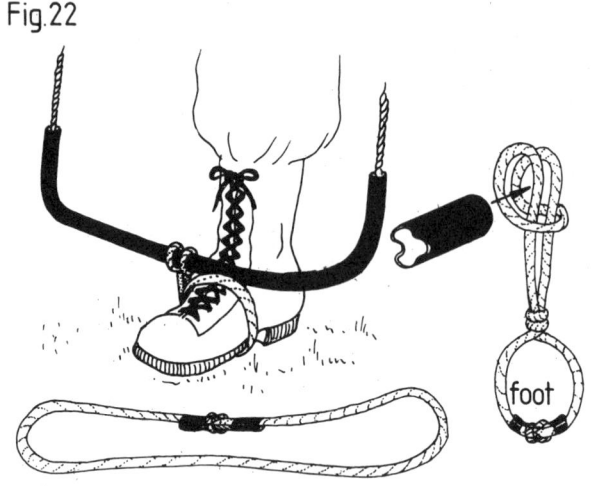

FIRST PRONE TAKE OFF. This will not be as dramatic as it sounds since we are going to take off with the harness virtually in the seated position, with the leg straps well up our thighs. The only difference will be a rather leaning-forward body attitude to cope with the forward bar position. No need to worry too much about the stirrup, just make sure the safety loop is secure. We've chosen a good soaring day so we will hardly have any take off run and we don't have to worry about it tripping us up. You will find this much less of a problem than you would expect. In well over 500 take-offs using a safety loop, I've never had a foul up and only missed the stirrup twice.

Once up and away we spend a couple of beats 'seated', getting as much height and distance out as we can. The first prone turn is going to be a completely new experience for which we need clear airspace. The intention is to get to one end, turn in the seated position and then rotate into prone as soon as we can. This will give us almost the whole beat to get used to it before we have to do our first prone turn.

We make the turn. This is it then . . . DON'T LOOK FOR THE STIRRUP . . . stretch out the loop leg and concentrate on flying the glider. Feel for the stirrup with your free foot and get it firmly in place ready to push. Concentrate on flying the glider . . . Now make a firm push on the stirrup (remember those leg straps are well up our thighs and need an extra effort to move). As this moves our weight forward in relation to our suspension point we rotate into the prone position almost automatically. Concentrate on flying the glider. Adjust airspeed. Wriggle the loop foot round onto the stirrup. If you get stuck go back to the seated position and land; don't try to sort it out in the air.

We try to look ahead and find it's near impossible, it feels as though we're trying to break our neck. Looking down is easy, sideways is not so bad, forwards is difficult, but upwards . . . no way! (You have to get used to turning the head sideways to look upward on each side in turn). Always remember that prone pilots have more 'blind spots' than seated pilots.

PRONE TURNS. We need to turn soon. The problem is to avoid pivoting, the head and shoulders going one way, the legs going the other with no real weight-shift relative to the glider. Start by pulling on a little speed and having a good look round in the direction of the turn. Now straighten the outside elbow and bend the inside one. This shifts the body and legs across *parallel with the keel.* The inside wing is loaded and the glider starts to turn. It feels very mechanical the first couple of times and it's no bad thing to pull in slightly with the bending arm as though to help look round the upright in the direction we are turning towards. As we do a few more and adjust to the new attitude we find it's more of a push with the outer arm and a collapsing on the inside one. This ensures that the legs don't lag behind. Once turning, we return to weight-shifting to co-ordinate speed and bank.

DO'S AND DON'TS. We try a few speed runs pulling ourselves further through the control frame each time. Neck and shoulder aches develop quickly. 15 mins is plenty for the first prone flight. Take her in and rotate back to seated at our old point A (Fig. 20). The approach should be exactly what we're used to except for the leaning forward position.

The greatest danger in prone flying is groping for a missed stirrup just after take off. The tendency is to look down for it and inadvertently push the bar forward. This inevitably risks a stall with no height to make a recovery. If you do miss the stirrup leave it where it is, keep looking ahead and around you. Climb steadily away, no matter how awkward you feel (and look). Sort it out when you have the height.

INSTRUMENTS. We will soon be able to tackle a wider range of conditions and find some thermals. We need to think about instruments. To maximise any advantage, we need to fly accurately, and for that we need an Airspeed Indicator (A.S.I.) We have seen how groundspeed can be a misleading reference at low level. At 1000ft, it, and many other ground features, cease to be any reference at all. Many pilots scorn an A.S.I., relying on the well established 'feel' they have for the glider. They have a point . . . that *'feel'* has to be acquired and retained but there are many circumstances when a glance at an A.S.I. can be very reassuring and enable us to cope better:

a) On a turbulent *downwind* approach for a landing.

b) On final descent for a top landing in light winds (to avoid overshooting).

c) Maintaining constant speed in turns at height when visibility is bad and we can't see the horizon. 'G' forces alter the feel and we can no longer rely on it.

d) Maximising surge lift in turbulence or small thermals when the tendency is to pull on speed before we need to.

e) Crossing hilly countryside when we need to fly at varying speeds accurately for considerable periods of lift and sink.

f) Detached from the glider it is an accurate wind speed indicator.

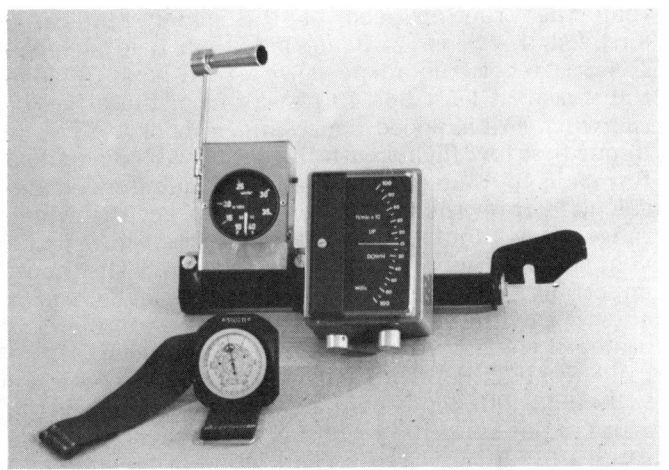

A WINTER airspeed indicator (left) and WILLIS variometer (right) mounted on a MAINAIR SPORTS instrument strut and bracket. In front a THOMMEN altimeter with wrist strap.

For any prolonged cross country flying a Variometer (Vario') and an altimeter are essential. Vario's measure slight pressure changes and convert them into 'going up' or 'going down' readings. The scale is normally in 100's ft per minute and we talk in terms of 'four up' or 'six down'. Some also have an audible signal in both directions. The type illustrated is only audible on 'up'. An altimeter is a particularly enjoyable instrument to have in all circumstances. There is great satisfaction in knowing exactly how high we are apart from it being essential for cross country flying.

Instruments, as a topic on their own, could fill a book. There are however a few basic facts we must know about them.

AIR SPEED INDICATORS. According to the position of the sensor the A.S.I. will register the speed of the airflow *at that point*. This is not the same as the speed of the glider through the air. Generally control frame mounted sensors will register a speed 2—3 mph slower than the true airspeed of the glider. (Indicated airspeed, I.A.S. is 2—3 mph less than true airspeed T.A.S.) To get true airspeed we would have to move the sensor at least 30—40ft away from the effect of the wing. (All airspeed figures in the book are T.A.S.) In our first few flights with the A.S.I. we have to do a few stalls to establish our *indicated* stalling speed and calculate from there. It takes time to get the whole range worked out but you'll be surprised how much your flying improves when you do. The most important requirement is that the speed can be *read at a glance* with sunglasses on or eyes watering. It's useless if you have to study it to read the speed.

VARIOMETERS. They can cost anywhere between £100 and £400. You get what you pay for. Don't be too attracted by sensitivity. Sensing every slight variation can lead to a bad case of 'the twitch' (a mental state where the pilot is convinced that his vario' is lying). We don't want to respond unless we hit a worth while 'up' or a sizeable 'down'. Most important is the zero control which is set at nil up or down before take off. It must be positive (not an easily disturbed knob) and it must be *stable* since it is almost impossible to reset it in flight. It must have an audible signal at least on 'up'. We may be working a thermal with others and needing to keep our eyes on them. (Always keep some spare long-life batteries in the flying bag; it's a lot of money to have idle).

ALTIMETERS. Cheap ones are a waste of money. Expect to pay at least £50. The Thommen (illustrated) is designed for climbers and is very good but there are others of similar style becoming available. Ex-RAF ones are excellent but a bit bulky.

Altimeters measure air pressure and will read higher as pressure drops. We have to reset them for each flight. For cross-countries where we may reach

3,000—4,000ft it is best set at 1013 milibars, the internationally agreed pressure at which all military and commercial aircraft set theirs. We must know our correct height, to fly within legal limits near controlled airspace.

Remember that whilst the Vario' gives us a whole string of 'ups' and 'downs' only the altimeter will tell us what they add up (or down) to.

O.K. got all that? . . . Let's go cross country!

CHAPTER 9
THERMAL FLYING CROSS COUNTRY

Once you have achieved your first cross country flight nothing will ever seem quite the same again.

What are thermals and how do they work? Air is not warmed directly by the sun. It is warmed when the ground or sea is warmer than itself. Since earth heats and cools quicker than water its effect on air is far greater. Put your hand on hard baked soil or tarmac on

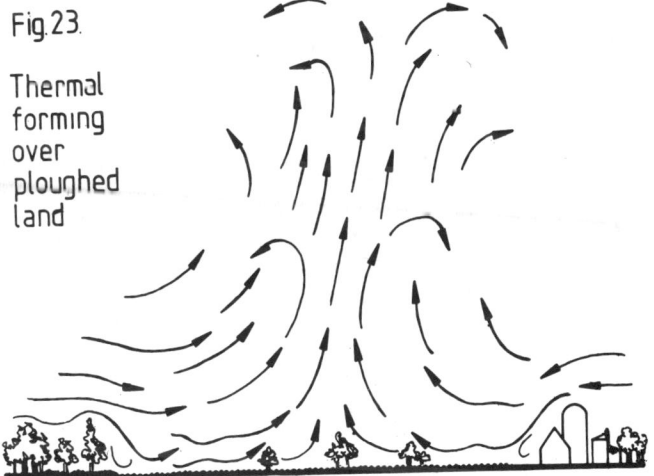

Fig. 23.

Thermal forming over ploughed land

only a moderately sunny day and you will be surprised how hot it is. Air passing slowly over such an area, ploughed fields, stubble, colliery tips, towns or bare south-facing slopes, is rapidly warmed. It begins to expand, its density is reduced and it starts to rise. Cooler air around it moves in underneath and may be warmed quickly enough for a rising column to develop.

If the replacement flow is not warmed quickly enough, because the 'warm spot' is small or the general air mass is moving too quickly, the thermal effect will be intermittent.

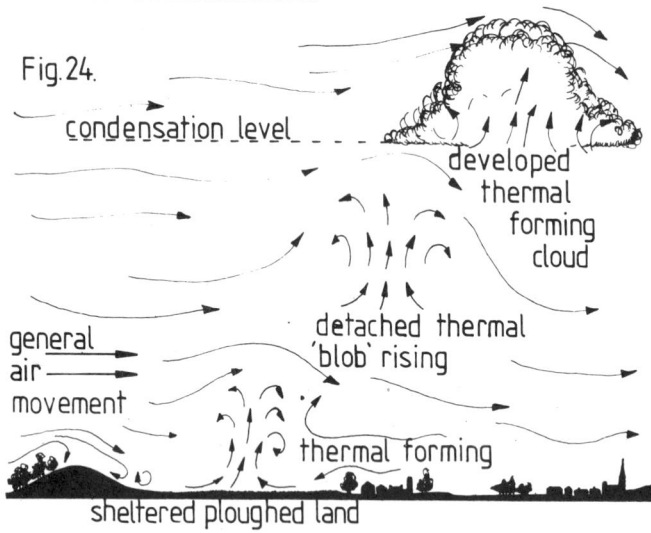

Fig. 24.

condensation level

developed thermal forming cloud

detached thermal 'blob' rising

general air movement

thermal forming

sheltered ploughed land

Once air starts to expand and rise it will go on doing so until it cools to the temperature of the surrounding air. In the lower atmosphere, air temperature reduces as you go up at approx. 2 deg. centigrade per 1000ft (6 deg. C per 1000 metres) but this is not constant. If the air is moist, clouds will form. The condensation releases latent heat which prolongs the thermal effect.

Occasionally, due to the earth cooling rapidly at night or the overlay of a differing air mass, temperatures can actually rise as you go up. We call this an INVERSION. It inhibits the development of thermals and you tend to get cloudless sky. Nice for the public but bad news for us.

Thermals come in all shapes and sizes. Some are small only 200—300ft across; some are large, 200—300 *yards* across. They can be weak or strong or have more than one core (main rising column of air). Under an inversion we get 'blue thermals' with no cloud forming. From a good source there can be 'standing column' thermals or intermittent 'blobs' popping off now and then. At condensation level these form lines of cotton wool clouds we call 'streets'. On cooler strong-winded days ridges tend to attenuate thermals; on light winded sunny days, bare south facing slopes can initiate or boost them.

This then, is the arena . . . now, let's play the game.

We are standing on a 500ft inland ridge. It is a late summer morning about 9.30 am. There is a gentle breeze, the sky is clear and the sun feels hot already. Upwind, stubble fields abound. The dew has lifted giving us patchy low cloud for an hour but this has now dispersed. Soon . . . there will be thermals!

Just after 10.30 somebody points excitedly. . . . a tiny wisp of cloud is beginning to form at about 2,500ft. It's starting to 'brew up'. By 11.00 am we are getting a few thermals coming through. The wind slackens to almost nothing as each approaches, drawing air in towards itself. After they pass we feel this effect increasing the wind speed which picks up to 14—15 mph. Thermals passing either side cause shifts in the wind direction as well.

We bide our time and watch the other pilots. They are biding their time and watching us. (Never be the first to go). We've only had our 'Super Ship' in the air three times and still don't believe we can take off in less than 10 mph and stay up (let alone 'hook' a thermal)!

Super Ace (every club has one) takes off in almost nil wind and zaps to and fro exchanging jocularities with the other 'hot shots'. Few of the words are intelligible but the message is plain enough . . . he ain't going up!

Suddenly we hear his vario' warble and he cranks in a quick 360 . . . he's away climbing steadily as he circles and slides back over the crest reaching 1,000ft in a couple of minutes. Two more take off and are 'scratching' level with take off. There is 'bad sink' and one goes down (oh, the shame); the other is well below the crest.

'Super Ace comes hurtling low over the ridge from behind'. His glider is a CYCLONE by Chargus Gliding Co. Ltd. of Buckingham. In the foreground is another of their designs, the VORTEX; its pilot is checking his harness.

Super Ace comes hurtling low over the ridge from behind, having decided that his first thermal wasn't worth staying with. His arrival coincides with the biggest thermal of the day so far (the one that was developing all that sink in front of it). In seconds he is climbing again with his vario 'off the clock'. (Of such luck is legend made). The other glider slots is underneath him and together they circle up until they are just tiny dots against the cloudbase. This has now risen to 3,500ft. (The condensation level usually rises as the day wears on). Cloud streets are forming everywhere. If we stand with our back to the wind we see that they do not align with the ground wind direction but swing away to the right. This is because the wind veers as you go up and can be as much as 45 degrees different at 5,000ft. Always keep this in mind when you study downwind terrain before going cross country.

The general opinion is that there are now 'plenty of good blobs to be had' and several gliders are 'skying out' at various heights . . . our moment has come!

All checks completed, we are poised in the take off area ready to launch. There is no more than a gentle 8—10 mph air movement barely filling the sail. It dies away completely . . . GO GO GO urge the other pilots waiting behind us . . . NO NO NO says our limited experience and we stay rooted waiting for it to pick up. (Mistake No. 1). We ignore the groans from behind.

It picks up to 12 mph . . . we go but miss the stirrup through running too hard, treating it more like a 'nil wind' than a normal take off (Mistake No. 2). By the time we've got is sorted we've lost height and really have to track in close to try and get it back. We keep our speed high (a little above Best L/D). The wind has obviously dropped again so we are not going to have any wind gradient problems. We've lost about sixty feet. We turn out to track back towards take off, converting a bit of that extra speed into not losing any height in the turn. As we approached flying, about 60ft out and 60ft down, so called friends shout various types of gleeful encouragement from the take off area

. . ."There's much more room higher up." (sarcastic). . . "Going down Bob?" (rhetorical) . . . "Come down and fetch you for a fiver." (optimistic). . . The swine!

We don't let it break our concentration; we've made two mistakes already, we don't want to make a third. We keep flying close and fast. We're not getting back up but we are not going down either. There's just enough lift to maintain height; we have to be ice cool and use every ounce of our skill. It's not all over.

In the next turn out we feel the lift increase slightly. The vario' gives a little quaarrk . . . we shorten our beat to get back to that end while it's still there. Half way back we start climbing . . . a glance at the A.S.I. confirms 20 mph (Best L/D edging towards Min Sink) and a steady quaaarrrr from the vario means '2 up' . . . OH BLISS . . . (see photo on page 89).

We let the turn broaden as we rise, passing back in front of take off. We leer down (smirk, smirk) and keep the turn going 360 degrees staying with the thermal lift all the way to come out about 200ft directly above. We hold it there in the best ridge lift and the vario goes silent. Damn! Lost it. (Thinking ridge, not thinking thermal). Still, we've got 200ft to play with and there are plenty of thermals coming through. Two gliders are climbing in something down the other end . . . we track that way to get in under them . . . nothing there . . . we're too late, it's left the ridge . . . well not quite, the tail end of it gives us another 100ft. Let's try out in front to give us time to see what each thermal is really worth before we are committed i.e. too far over the back to get forwards and onto the ridge face again.

We head out and hit bad sink '4 down'. We increase speed to get through it as quickly as possible . . . WHAM, rising air hits us with a strap-wrenching surge. Queeeeeeeeaaaaarrrrrr, the vario' peaks at '8 up' dropping back to '5' . . . we're into one that was bang on the nose . . . are we in the middle? . . . Which way to turn? . . . Try right, she seems to want to go that way (Mistake No. 3) . . . As we let her turn, up goes the left wing and down goes the nose with alarming rapidity...

'... OH BLISS ...' Cloud formations in the background show us Fig. 24 in reality as Tony Beresford prepares to depart on his CHEROKEE from Birdman of Mildenhall.

we pull on speed, get the wings level and pull out . . . good job no one else was too close . . . WE WUZ SPEWED (literally tossed out or flew out of the side of a strongly developed thermal).

Now that is three mistakes! Lets stop muckin' about. Lets start flyin' right and grab us a piece o' this 'ere sky!

The altimeter is reading 1200ft A.S.L. (above sea level). We set it at ridge height 500ft before taking off, so we have 700ft above take off. Doesn't everybody look small way down there. We head out again about a quarter of a mile, we don't have to worry about the lift band at this height . . . THIS . . . is FREEDOM. The glider wobbles and the left wing lifts slightly . . . something that side? . . . we turn towards it . . . a couple of '360's . . . nothing but steady '2' down! our normal rate of descent. Well we're not in sink, so keep going parallel to the ridge and well out. We have height and patience and that's all we need.

Bad sink . . . '6 down' . . . something's near but which way? Try left . . . she doesn't want to go . . . this could be it . . . pull on speed and make a really "heavy" weight shift to roll her against the resistance. We cut into it and start climbing '4 up' . . . ease the turn, let's really "suss" (cautiously and thoroughly investigate) this one. As the turn broadens the vario' drops to '2 up', no good, got to tighten the turn and find that 'core'. We're only on the edge of it yet. '4 up' . . . keep the turn going . . . this one's enormous . . . queeeeeeeeeeeeeeeee . . . the vario' hits the stop '10 up' . . . ease the turn, that must have been the 'core' so settle back into a smooth 360 at 18 mph. Let's not vary the bank and pitch too much; we want to be sure that what we are getting on the vario' is from the thermal, not from control movements. We keep making minor corrections in the turn, tightening it a little as the lift decreases, easing it as the lift increases, getting about an average '5 up'. In two or three minutes we are well behind the ridge and looking along the cloudbase. *Along* the cloudbase!

We look at the altimeter. 2,900ft!

We've still got the thermal nicely 'centred'; our turn is keeping us in it even though the lift is not quite so strong now, '4 up'. The cloud looms only 200ft above, the ground looks miles away, cars are tiny dots, people are difficult to distinguish.

'. . . the groung looks miles away . . .' Keith Reynolds on his SIGMA (seen taking off in Chap. 1) has now 'hooked' a good 'blob' over Lachens in the south of France at the 1980 Bleriot Cup.

"Shall we split?"

"You mean go for it?"

A last lingering look at the ridge we know so well . . .
our eyes turn downwind to the distant horizon . . . a
little to our surprise we find the glider has turned with
them . . . THIS IS IT!

We keep circling under 'our' cloud and drift gently
downwind. A steady '2 up' takes us into the arch of it's
base which is far from flat. It's much easier to 'centre'
the thermal now we can see it. About four miles
downwind the vario' goes silent (a tiny crack appears
in our self confidence). Think carefully, a zero reading
means we are still in good lift (anything less than '2
down' is lift). *Never leave lift.* Hang in there as long as
it lasts, we're still making distance and that's what we
came for. We keep circling in lazy 360's at 18—20 mph.
Five miles now, over the back of the high ground and
above the downslope, the vario' has died, not a squeak
out of it for the last 5 minutes, a steady '1 down'.
Altimeter 3,400ft.

The cloud is beginning to look a bit ragged (decaying)
and it's becoming decidedly chilly. Let's work out to
'the sunny side of the street'. Circling out into
sunshine we get '1 up'. Good move. No point in
circling any more; why not fly along the edge of the
cloud street in the sunshine? The ridge is seven miles
behind us now and we have time to admire the view.
What's that road below? Must be the B road from the
site . . . yes there's the Rose and Crown (good spot to
land) . . . not this time . . . our eyes follow the road
looking for the Motorway; if we can cross that we'll
have done nine miles. Yes there it is . . . we'll make it,
no problem.

The vario' is silent again. The clouds are beginning to
look more like flat pancakes. 2—3 more miles
downwind they are disappearing altogether. We are
getting '2 down' as we cross the motorway and could
perhaps make another 3 to 4 miles on glide angle.
Altimeter 2,200ft (about 2,000ft ground clearance) . . .
Let's not push our luck. The large town of Sinchester

lies directly in our path, considerably surrounded by an assortment of wooded areas and POWER LINES. What if we hit sink over the woods? (These are not the thoughts of a seasoned cross country pilot, you appreciate, they are, however, the thoughts of one likely to become seasoned).

Two large fields by a farmhouse offer the opportunity to set up for an easy approach and landing. They look flat (they are not) and free of power lines, both the big pylon type and the smaller telegraph pole type you don't see till the last minute. Some distant smoke from straw-burning indicates the wind direction so we can enjoy the descent without having to worry about which way to line up into wind . We make big lazy circles to lose height, savouring every moment, checking drift and studying the fields. It's not until we are below 500ft that their unevenness becomes apparent. We'll have to go in slightly cross-winded to land uphill. At 200ft we put in our last crosswind leg along the edge of our chosen field. Dead into wind, it slopes down away from us towards the farmhouse. We'll have to line up going uphill towards the gate about 45 degrees out of wind . . . the other field would have been better. (This is always the case regardless of which field you choose). At 100ft we pull on speed and turn in for our landing. Once we are clearly over any obstructions and into the field we increase speed and almost dive for the ground. Remember, there can be all sorts of turbulence and wind gradient in so called sheltered spots. Never come in slow. When judging approaches to strange landing areas always keep a bit high and a bit fast. *We can't stretch our best glide angle, we can only shorten it.* If we have speed and are heading straight for an obstruction it can be converted into height and we can probably clear it. Don't leave it too late and get caught by a rotor.

We judge it fairly well, there's very little wind at ground level so we don't have to contend with a lot of drift, and touch down 60 yds from the gate. Must be 10 miles at least! (By some strange phenomenon the

Ordnance Survey always make it less). Others, we learn, did 15 and 20 miles but much later in the day. It must have gone on getting better, perhaps we went too soon.

A car has stopped, some people are coming into the field from the lane.

"Can little Christopher have his photo taken by the glider?"

"Certainly little Christopher can have his photo taken by the glider. Would little Christopher like to wear our helmet for the photo?"

"We've been watching you for miles. Where have you come from?"

"Hanging Down by Little Bedstead actually."

"Oh yes we've seen them *there* but we didn't realise you could fly *anywhere*. You must be one of the experts."

"Well . . ."

"Can we give you a lift back?"

What a wonderful world . . . What lovely people . . . You relax in the passenger seat (your mind still at 2,000ft) hearing those magic words over and over again . . . "We didn't know you could fly *anywhere*. You must be one of the *experts*."

CHAPTER 10
POWERED HANG GLIDERS

This is one facet of Microlight Aviation i.e. aircraft having an unladen weight below the limit set by The Civil Aviation Authority (under revision 1981). Many of these have conventional three axis aerodynamic controls, (elevators, ailerons and rudders). This chapter deals only with the application of power units to weight shift/flexwing gliders and what this offers the prospective pilot.

Early development was almost entirely confined to keel hung power units. Although a 200 mile and several cross Channel flights were achieved, there were serious drawbacks in foot launching and handling the high thrust line in turbulent conditions.

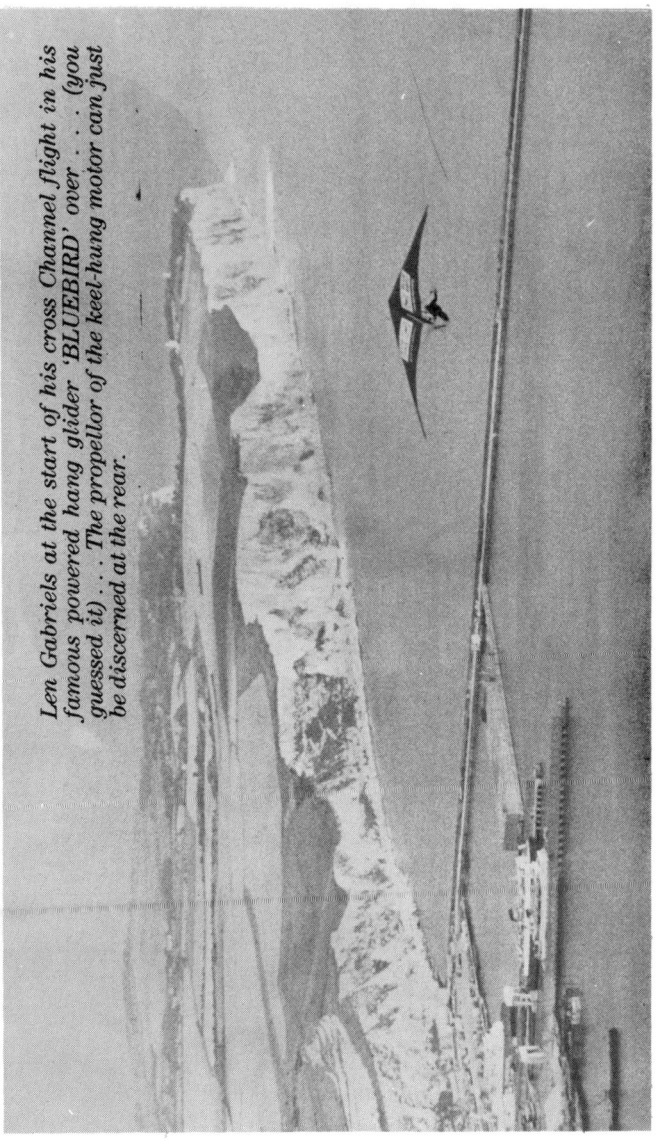

Len Gabriels at the start of his cross Channel flight in his famous powered hang glider 'BLUEBIRD' over . . . (you guessed it) . . . The propellor of the keel-hung motor can just be discerned at the rear.

A development combination. The Skyhook SILHOUETTE with their own 'Trike' attached.

It was not until the conception of the 'Trike' configuration that Powered Hang Gliding became a real option for the average pilot. Today's high performance Gliders are all manufactured and sold with a Powered Trike option.

If you haven't got any good hills near you or you don't like climbing them anyway, the power option is very attractive. There's no doubt that without power you have to be out on the hills at every likely opportunity if you want to fly cross country more than two or three times a year. With power, even an average pilot can cruise the same sky a good deal more frequently with the added advantage that he can probably fly back again as well.

There is a price to pay (there always is). Even the simplest engine/airframe needs experience and skill to maintain. The sort of neglect you give your car (be honest now) could kill you. The aim is for *complete* reliability. Bear in mind, your power unit will be an adapted and modified air cooled industrial two-stroke engine not a 'twin magneto, heated carburettor, supercharged aero engine.' It will not be difficult to look after but you will need to set up a regular maintenance and routine renewal schedule i.e. change the plug and clean the points etc. *before* they fail. You might find it difficult to do afterwards. Anyone who has not experienced an engine failure in flight has one of life's 'less treasured moments' still to come.

A powered aircraft is very vulnerable immediately after take off. Unlike a ridge-launched glider it doesn't get an instant 200—300ft ground clearance to play with. Most schools now operate from conventional airfields and this is where the complete newcomer to flying must start. Even an experienced Hang Glider pilot would prefer to make his first couple of flights (at least) where the opportunity to land back from any height is always there. It is even possible to survive a dreaded 'downwind landing' without damage (provided you keep her straight).

You will probably start in a two seater machine. After one or two dual flights, some taxi-ing instruction

The DEMON/SKYTRIKE combination from Hiway Hang Gliders, one of the most popular models in series production 1980/81.

and one or two solo 'ground hops' you will progress through 'circuits and bumps' to free flying. There is a lot to learn (apart from flying). Rigging, starting up, warming up (never take off with a cold engine), fault detection, propellor discipline, pre-flight checks, taxiing etc. etc. Powered flying is no short cut to the sky.

Depending on your requirement the engine can be no more than auxiliary 'flight sustainer' or a more powerful 'flight maker'. The drag of a 'Trike' is about double that of a prone pilot but attached to one of the new 60% double surface wings, glide angles are better than 8—1 and descent rates (power off) are between 250—300ft per min. Climbing speeds on full power are between 30 and 35 mph, gliding speeds about the same. Maximum level flight speeds are between 50 and 60 mph according to your power unit. The following table is an approximate indication of the current options.

Engine Capacity Cubic Centimetres	Maximum Static Thrust. (lbs)	Approx. Rate of climb in still air (ft. per min).
150	100	200
250	150	400
350 (twin cylinder)	200	600

It will be obvious from Chapter 3 that there are many situations where, even with full power on, you would still be going down. Your cruising speed is between 35 and 45 mph. Control capability in turbulence is less than a glider, although your initial stability is greater. You have considerable limitations. Wind speeds increase as you go up. You would find any prolonged flight into a strong headwind simply not worth the effort.

The tendency is to choose 'lighter' conditions and those beautiful sunny nil-wind days we all used to dread before power was available. What more has life to offer than trundling down to the airfield, wheeling out the old 'kite', whisking it up to 3000ft, cutting the power, doing a spot o' thermaling, enjoying the view and back down for a pint and a chat. Did that sound a little nostalgic perhaps? The phraseology of yesteryear? Well, I make no apology for the fact that we have only just re-discovered the aeroplane. The difference this time is that anyone who wants to fly one and is physically able, can do it for less than half the price of a second-hand car.

The Civil Aviation Authority has introduced regulations for Microlight power flying. With effect from 30th September, 1981, you will need to qualify for a Pilot's licence by passing a recognised test and obtain an annual flying permit. You will also need a Medical Certificate. For further details contact the British Microlight Aircraft Association (Secretary 1981, R. M. Bott, 20 Church Hill, Ironbridge, Telford, Shropshire TF8 7PZ).